MW00981845

GOLDEN NUGGETS

Roadhouse Portraits along the Cariboo's Gold Rush Trail

Branwen Patenaude

CANADIAN CATALOGUING IN PUBLICATION DATA

Patenaude, Branwen C. (Branwen Christine), 1927-
Golden Nuggets

Includes bibliographical references and index.
ISBN 1-895811-56-2

1. Taverns (Inns)—British Columbia—Cariboo (Regional district)—Pictorial works
2. Taverns (Inns)—British Columbia—Cariboo (Regional district)—History
3. Cariboo (B.C.: Regional district)—Gold discoveries
4. Cariboo (B.C.: Regional district)—History
I. Title

FC3822.5.P384   1998   971.1'75   C98-910123-1   F1089.C3P38   1998

First Edition 1998

Heritage House wishes to acknowledge the the Department of Canadian Heritage through the Book Publishing Industry Development Program, the Canada Council, and the British Columbia Arts Council for supporting various aspects of its publishing program. We also wish to acknowledge the valuable services provided by the British Columbia Archives and Records Service (BCARS) to enhance the visual presentation of this book.

Cover, book design, typesetting and maps: Darlene Nickull
Edited by: Joanne Richardson

HERITAGE HOUSE PUBLISHING COMPANY LTD.
Unit #8 - 17921 55th Ave., Surrey, BC, V3S 6C4

Printed in Canada

Front Cover
Cottonwood House (upper), a roadhouse between Quesnel and Wells in 1995. The photo shows a replica of an 1870s *BX* stagecoach driven by Frank Thiel and his son. Standing from left to right are Kimberly Patenaude and her father David Patenaude. To the right and holding the horses is gold miner Wilf Patenaude. Soda Creek, B.C. c. 1865 (bottom). On the one street are seen the two roadhouses, P. Dunlevy's "Exchange" hotel, and R. McLeese's "Colonial Hotel."

Back Cover
Top row left to right: Ashcroft Manor, Quesnel Forks; and S. Prior's "Little Lake House."
Second row: Frank Mooney's cabin, Quesnel River; Cariboo Gold Quartz Mine.
Third row: Chinese Masonic Lodge, Barkerville; Fosters Bar, Fraser River.
Fourth row: Cottonwood House, W.J. Anders House, and the last roadhouse on the Keithley Ranch.
Middle picture: Catholic Church, Pavilion, B.C.

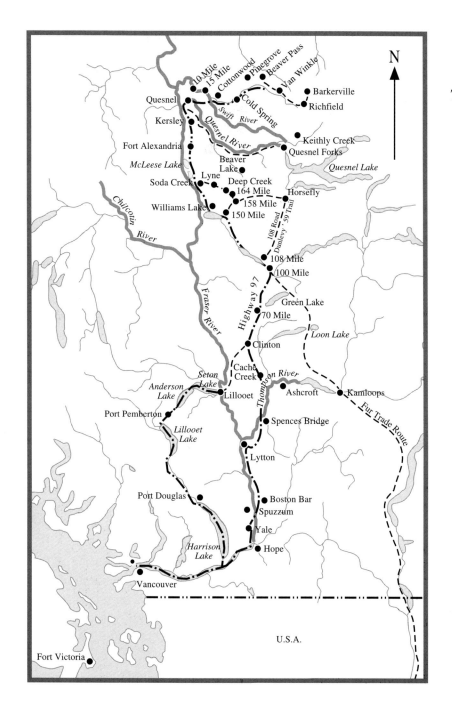

Contents

Introduction

In order to find the best wagon-road route to the goldfields, surveys were made and roads were built (and, in some cases, changed several times) before the Cariboo Wagon Road finally reached Barkerville on Williams Creek in 1865. Over a century later no fewer than eight original roadhouses from that colourful era are still to be found spread across the landscape, wherever the several roads or trails to the Cariboo were built and wherever travellers needed shelter and food.

Frederick Dally, 1868

When Branwen Patenaude began her research on the roadhouses of the Cariboo, she undertook a massive task. Out of her study came documentation on over 180 such establishments. This work has been published in two separate volumes of *Trails to Gold* and contains almost 500 pages of detail.

To understand the gold-rush trail one has to appreciate the BC landscape. In March of 1858, when 10,000 California miners arrived at the mouth of the Fraser River, they found gold 100 miles upstream — as far as Fort Yale, a Hudson's Bay Company (HBC) supply post. Beyond that, and for the next ten miles, two dangerous canyons made travel upstream virtually impossible. In the meantime, reports were heard of larger gold finds on the benches above Lytton and at Lillooet, 60 miles upstream.

The California miners at Yale had not counted on the annual spring run-off of the Fraser River, which from April until mid-August covered all the rich mining ground. Impatient outcries soon reached the ears of the government, and by June 500 miners were employed in the building of a 65-mile road from Port Douglas, at the head of Harrison Lake, through a series of portages and lakes to Lillooet.

By blasting the canyons above Yale in 1861, the Royal Engineers made way for a road, and by the next spring work had commenced on two routes. The most ambitious was charted from Yale through the Fraser Canyon to Lytton, up the Thompson River to Spences Bridge, and north to Clinton. The other, awarded to Gustavus B. Wright, was charted along a difficult 47-mile route from Lillooet to Clinton. As time was of the essence, the government demanded that the contracts be completed expeditiously. When the builders of the Yale route failed to deliver, their contract was cancelled. In the meantime, G.B. Wright's road reached Clinton in August of 1862, and he was then given a mandate to build an additional 130-plus miles of road north to Alexandria. The building of the Yale Road, which was finally completed in 1863, soon led to the phasing out of the inefficient, portage-ridden Harrison-Lillooet route.

Despite a scandal over the route of the Cariboo Road at Williams Lake, G.B. Wright's road reached Alexandria in August of 1863. However, completion of this contract still left the 35 miles to Quesnel without a road. Despite the government's call for tenders, no one applied, least of all G.B. Wright and his associates, who had built the SS *Enterprise*, a sternwheel riverboat that began operations that summer, carrying passengers and freight up the Fraser River between Soda Creek and Quesnel.

Golden Nuggets is a portrayal of the people, the events, and the roadhouses of the Cariboo gold-rush era. This publication has been developed to complement *Trails to Gold* and as a companion to Art Downs's hugely popular *Wagon Road North*.

We owe a debt of gratitude to Frederick Dally (above) and to both the professional and amateur photographers of the nineteenth century for the images they have given us of the early days along the Cariboo Wagon Road and the many "trails to gold" portrayed in this book.

Yale: Gateway to Gold

One of the earliest and most lucrative of enterprises in British Columbia was roadhouse keeping. With the arrival of thousands of prospectors and gold miners on the lower Fraser River in the early spring of 1858 came the immediate need for shelter, food, lodging for animals, and stores.

The earliest roadhouse on record was that of Thomas York at Yale, 100 miles from the mouth of the Fraser River. While the first miners travelled upriver in their own conveyances, later arrivals travelled by sternwheel steamship to Yale, the northern terminus.

The earliest restaurants and hotels in communities such as Yale were crude log shacks, no more sophisticated than their counterparts along the wilderness trails of the Interior, and they provided only the bare necessities of life. Prior to the building of roads and the use of stagecoaches, each of these public facilities contained only a single room and a sleeping loft.

It was not long before several hotels and restaurants opened at Yale along the one street facing the waterfront. Three of the more popular of these were Captain William Power's Hotel and Restaurant, the Colonial Hotel (built in 1862 by Perrier and Latremouillere), and California House.

This 1865 photo (left) documents a visit by the SS Lillooet, which had been launched in 1863 for Captain J.R. Fleming. For a period it wore antlers atop its wheelhouse, this being symbolic of its status as the Fraser River's speed champion. The church in the background and inset is St. John the Divine, built in 1860, the oldest church in British Columbia still operating on its original site.

On July 4, 1867, Canada was three days old, but this seems the most likely date for this Front Street photo of Yale (bottom). Many of Yale's occupants were transplanted Americans. At least two "stars-and-stripes" flags are flying, and an unmarked sternwheeler (likely the Hope) sits empty as the streets are aflood with midday celebrants.

From Yale to Barkerville, the history of the gold-rush pioneers produces an endless portrait of honest, determined adventurers who helped settle British Columbia. Upper left, Captain William Power operated the best hotel in Yale in 1858, and, lower left, Napolean Latremouillere was co-owner of the Colonial Hotel. Latremouillere and his partner later moved their operations to Barkerville.

David W. Higgins (right), a journalist from Nova Scotia, came to Yale via the Fraser River in 1858. By coincidence, he arrived on the same sternwheeler, the *Enterprise*, as did Captain William Power. Higgins would go on to own Victoria's *Colonist* newspaper; serve as speaker in the BC Legislature; and, in two popular turn-of-the-century memoirs, pen stories of his adventures. In one of these stories he describes his first encounter with Captain Power. Higgins recognized Power as "a splendid specimen of manhood," and his record of their conversation (below) seems consistent with Power's portrait.

From David Higgins's short story, "Jem McLaughlin's Transformation," which describes the author's first meeting with William Power.

I had met him early one sunny morning in August 1858, on the saloon deck of Captain Thomas Wright's sternwheel steamer *Enterprise*, as she ploughed slowly against the current on her way to Hope. I had risen early and was reading a book when I saw approaching me a tall, fair young man. He held in one hand what seemed to be a China mug. As he drew near he said: "I've been all over this precious craft looking for the steward. Do you know where he is to be found?"

I replied in the negative, adding that I was, like himself, a stranger on board.

"I want some hot water," he said. "I've travelled all over Europe and the Holy Land and have been on the Nile, but this is the first time I have found it impossible to get a cup of hot water to shave with. What do you use?"

I told him I used cold water.

"If I've got to use cold water," he replied, "I'll not shave at all," and he didn't for several years.

From *Tales of a Pioneer Journalist*, D.W. Higgins.

As news of the riches at Hill's Bar, just downstream from Yale, reached San Francisco, a large population from all walks of life, including a segment of undesirables, quickly made its way to the new bonanza. By early 1859 the little community had become both a boomtown and a hellhole (the latter status due to there being too few representatives of the law).

There were, however, many upstanding and reputable citizens of Yale, particularly amongst the permanent residents. An example of these were the three Nelson brothers: Hugh, as the junior partner in the firm of Deitz and Nelson, the successors to William Ballou's Express Company; Mard, who later owned several roadhouses on the Cariboo Road; and Uriah, who operated a packing and forwarding agency in Port Douglas and became a successful merchant in Yale, Clinton, and Ashcroft.

By 1864 Francis J. Barnard was operating a four-horse stagecoach service from Yale up the new Cariboo Road via Ashcroft and Clinton to Soda Creek. One of the first drivers on this route was James Hamilton, who drove from Clinton to Lac La Hache. Hamilton later became a partner in the BC Express Company.

Below, from left to right: Uriah Nelson, Francis J. Barnard, and James Hamilton. Bottom, a BC Express stagecoach loaded and ready to leave Ashcroft, c. 1890.

Also known as the Great Canyon, Hell's Gate remains a popular attraction now served by an air tramway.

Upon their arrival on the Fraser River in March of 1858, miners found rich deposits of fine gold as they made their way upriver. On reaching Yale, they were in for a surprise. Little did they realize that the annual snowmelt would cause the Fraser drainage system to rise to dramatic heights, preventing access to all the rich mining bars until later in the summer.

Then word reached Yale that other miners, who had travelled overland to Lytton and Lillooet 60 miles upstream from Yale, were extracting larger nuggets and bigger quantities of gold from the benches above the river. To reach Lillooet became the aim of every miner who faced the obstacle of the Fraser Canyon in the summer of 1858.

As the waters rose, travel upstream on the Fraser River became impossible. Not only was it a life-threatening experience to pass through the canyons, but hostile Natives residing in the area were, in many instances, ambushing and killing the miners, decapitating them before throwing them into the river.

The invasion of the American miners had quite naturally upset the Natives, who saw their domain being threatened, their rights being ignored, and Native women being abused. At this point Natives were not even being allowed to mine for gold.

At Hell's Gate Canyon, also known as the Upper Canyon, the miners and the Natives of the region fought a three-day battle at the end of August 1858. Upon the completion of negotiations and settlements with at least a dozen Native bands up and down the river, the miners were allowed to return to their claims on the Fraser River.

In this early painting, an unknown artist portrays local Natives on their traditional fishing grounds at Hell's Gate.

The Harrison Route: Port Douglas to Lillooet

In May of 1858, with an impassable Fraser River and hostile Native bands in the Upper Canyon, an arrangement between the miners and the government helped turn an old HBC trading route into the new trail inland. Governor Douglas recruited 500 miners and made it possible for a trail to be built to Lillooet by way of Port Douglas at the head of Harrison Lake. Completed by fall, the four-foot-wide path followed a trail well known to the HBC. As many as twelve roadhouses operated along the 65-mile route between 1858 and 1865.

The new route invited more competition among freighters, and rates dropped by over 60 percent. Port Douglas flourished until the completion of the road through the Fraser Canyon and, at its peak, contained every conceivable business of the time — even a wagon-making factory. Wagons were used to transport goods to Bridge River north of Lillooet after a rich strike of gold was discovered there.

The remains of the hotel at Port Douglas stand behind a cairn marking the beginning of the Port Douglas-to-Lillooet trail at the top of Harrison Lake.

Port Douglas flourished until 1864 and then gradually fell into disrepair. This photo was taken from a sternwheeler in 1895.

To reach the start of the Lillooet trail, passengers boarded a sternwheeler from New Westminster and travelled up the Fraser and Harrison Rivers to the mouth of Harrison Lake, a large, deep body of water 45 miles long. Three steamers built to carry miners up the lake from the Harrison's mouth were the SS *Marzelle*, the SS *Seton*, and the SS *Prince of Wales*, a later vessel. At the far end, on a short spit of land, stood the town of Port Douglas.

Among the many travellers on the Port Douglas-to-Lillooet trail in 1863 were Dr. W.B. Cheadle and Lord Milton, who spent nights at many of the crude, early roadhouses. A journal of their travels was published in 1865. It contains several sketches depicting typical conditions in the early roadhouses, where miners rolled up in their blankets on dirt floors and where the only sources of heat, light, and cooking were the open fireplaces.

The first seven roadhouses on the trail were built between Port Douglas and 29 Mile House, beside Little Lillooet Lake. This was the southern terminus of the steamboats that operated between here and Port Pemberton. In 1863 the 29 Mile House was operated

by Joseph L. Smith and his partner Thomas Marshall. These entrepreneurs owned several of the early roadhouses along the Harrison route. By 1868 they had settled in Clinton, where they bought the Clinton Hotel and where they remained for many years.

"Midnight in a Roadhouse," lithograph (top) taken from Dr. W.B. Cheadle's Northwest Passage by Land, *1865. The roadhouse was located at 29 Mile Landing (left), on the Harrison route north of Port Douglas. A sternwheel steamer is tied up at the 29 Mile House landing (below).*

Demise of the Harrison Route

Lord Milton and Dr. W.B. Cheadle took this route in 1863, and their journals were later published as memoirs. They spoke well of Ketterel's Halfway House between Lillooet and Anderson Lakes. Two years later, photographer Charles Gentile would capture the charm of this roadhouse with his Barkerville-bound lens.

In 1861 both Bishop George Hills and Dr. Cheadle commented on the appeal of Seton Lake. Cheadle thought it the most beautiful scenery of his trip, and Hills mentioned both a roadhouse and a steamboat. Although some establishments stubbornly hung on into the twentieth century, many shelters along this route fell into ruin.

Seen here in the 1880s, the SS Britannia *(top right) was the last steamboat to provide service on Seton Lake.*

Seton House (right), seen here as it was in the 1940s, is thought to have been the site referenced in Bishop Hills's journal 80 years earlier.

This 1865 Gentile photo of Ketterel's Halfway House (below) is representative of the many quality compositions he brought back from his trip to the Cariboo.

Alexandra Bridge to Lytton and Lillooet: Following the Fraser River

At Spuzzum, a point on the Fraser River about eleven miles northeast of Yale, an American, Franklin Way, received a contract to operate a ferry across the river in 1858. From the east bank a trail built by miners led upriver to Boston Bar and Lytton. With his contract in hand, Frank also built a roadhouse close to the ferry. The large population heading upriver at that time kept Frank's ferry and roadhouse very busy, and for a few years he did a roaring business.

In 1860, with partner Josiah C. Beedy of Yale, Frank also took a contract to build a mule trail along the mountain from Yale to Spuzzum. This trail was completed in September, and it prompted further development of a road through the canyon — a road that, ironically, eventually put Frank Way out of business.

While at Yale in October of 1861, Governor Douglas discussed the feasibility of building a wagon road along this route to Lytton and from there up the Thompson River to Cook's Ferry, known today as Spences Bridge. With the expertise of the Royal Engineers, the route was surveyed and the rocks of the canyon were blasted to start making room for a road to the Interior. At this time a party of Royal Engineers under the command of Sergeant William McColl was sent to find a site at which to build a bridge across the Fraser. The site chosen was close to Frank Way's ferry. Anticipating the end to his enterprise at Spuzzum, Frank sold out to Thomas York of Yale.

In 1863 Joseph Trutch took a contract to build a bridge across the Fraser River at Spuzzum. With a span of over 300 feet, this was the first suspension bridge built in British Columbia. Named the Alexandra Bridge, after Princess Alexandra of Great Britain, it was completed in September of 1864 at a cost of $45,000. In the 1920s the provincial government allowed the original bridge to be demolished. True, it was in need of repair, but save for the decking, which had been allowed to rot and which could have been replaced at nominal cost, it was structurally sound. A second bridge, which still stands on the original site, was built in 1927.

Below is the first suspension bridge in British Columbia. It was built across the Fraser River at Spuzzum in 1864. Sergeant William McColl of the Royal Engineers (inset) chose the site of the Alexandra Bridge.

Alexandra Lodge

Situated beside Highway 97 twelve miles north of Yale is Alexandra Lodge, parts of which are said to be over 100 years old. Known originally as Chapman's Bar House, the name altered over time due to its proximity to the Alexandra Bridge just north of Spuzzum. Below is a classic photograph of the lodge, taken by Frederick Dally in 1867, as well as one of how it appears today (inset).

Twenty miles north of Boston Bar, Dally also captured this roadhouse scene at Boothroyd's 210-acre homestead at the peak of its glory (below). With time, brothers George and William Boothroyd had a major falling out. George, with his Native wife and a family of nine (inset photo), moved to Victoria in 1873. William lost the ranch via foreclosure three years later and returned to England.

The Fearsome Fraser Canyon

The actual building of the road started early in 1862, with the first seven miles being built by the Royal Engineers. These scenes of China Bar Bluff north of Yale and the wagon road at the summit of Jackass Mountain were taken by Frederick Dally in July of 1867, when he travelled with Governor Seymour's party on a trip to the Cariboo. The poles seen in the pictures carried the telegraph lines, which were established in 1865.

George Salter's roadhouse and outbuildings at the 42 milepost in the Fraser Canyon (as photographed by Dally) were located on a small bench of land at the foot of Jackass Mountain. Built in 1861 the facility catered mostly to freighters, who sometimes lodged there for several days while they drove their loaded wagons up the steep, long hill. Salter sold out in 1873 to William A. Johnston, a later pioneer of Quesnel. Roadhouse keepers found it most profitable to build either at the top or the bottom of a long hill. This was because it took a long time and a lot of work to get the freight wagons up and down the many steep hills in the area.

China Bar Bluff (top left) and the Fraser Canyon near Jackass Mountain (top right) depict the road during its early years. The middle photo shows how the road was later disrupted by the building of the Canadian Pacific Railway.

Salter's 42 Mile House in the Fraser Canyon (bottom). This roadhouse later became an Anglican Church mission, where Priests Edwards and Small taught local Native boys.

The rugged canyon made for slow going, and in the early 1860s there were at least four roadhouses between Boston Bar (aptly named after a group of early miners with Massachusetts origins) and Kanaka Bar.

With the wagon road being built through the community of Boston Bar in 1862, Alexander Coutlie, an American entrepreneur, established the International Hotel (seen here in 1880). Alex's inn was highly regarded until the government got involved. In 1866 Coutlie was forced to pay for his pre-empted land and was charged $200 for an annual operating licence. These costs forced him to sell.

This was the first site of Boston Bar, and it was close to the Fraser River. Following serious flooding in the spring of 1894, the site was moved to a higher bench to the north.

The coming of the Canadian Pacific Railway (CPR) through the canyon in the 1880s disrupted sections of the wagon road in deference to the needs of the "iron horses." Still, it remained a vital link to the Interior, and sections of the original road remained in use for many decades. Prior to the widening of Highway 97 through the Fraser Canyon in the 1940s, wooden platforms hung out over the canyon walls, as seen in this 1919 photograph taken at the summit of Jackass Mountain. Fortunately, most early cars were light and could be lifted over to one side upon meeting another vehicle. During the winter, and after a heavy fall of snow, the road would be blocked, sometimes for many days.

When gold was discovered by Hawaiians at this point on the Fraser River in 1858, it became known as Kanaka Bar. By 1860 two French miners, Eugene Combe and Charles Sadoux, took up land and opened a roadhouse here. They also sent a request to France for alfalfa seed and soon had a crop to feed stage horses and freight teams. For many years this was a very lively spot on the Cariboo Road, with freighters bringing supplies to the roadhouse and the BC Express stagecoach coming to the door. It was also here that some of British Columbia's first tobacco was grown. The remains of the Kanaka Bar House (c. 1920) are seen at the left.

Louis Vincent Hautier and his wife Josephine Dubois Vanderbrook Hautier (insets), operators of the pioneer Globe Hotel.

This photograph of the village of Lytton was taken by Charles Gentile in 1865. At first known as "the Forks," where the Thompson River flows into the Fraser, Lytton was the scene of wild activity in 1858 when gold was first discovered on the high benches above the river. Note the French flag flying above the single street of the little community. There was a large number of French settlers in the area, many of whom had been associated with the HBC prior to the gold rush.

The Hautiers and the Globe Hotel

In 1860, driven by dreams of wealth and opportunity, Belgian immigrant Louis Vincent Hautier and his wife Josephine travelled with their two small children from Victoria to Lytton. Reaching Yale by steamboat, they walked the final 60 miles accompanied by Native bearers and a Native woman named Lasha, who carried baby Alphonse and helped three-year-old Louisa along the trail. Lasha remained as the Hautiers' nurse for many years.

The Hautiers acquired land in the new townsite and opened the Globe Hotel in 1862. Josephine, who had been a professional opera singer in Victoria, was a gourmet cook and supervised the kitchen at the hotel, which, for many years, had the indisputable reputation of serving the best meals on the Cariboo Wagon Road.

Through the ups and downs of their tenure at Lytton, the Hautiers raised five children, and when Louis and Josephine retired to their farm at Kanaka Bar in 1880, their eldest sons, Alphonse and Albert, took over the hotel. The original Globe Hotel burned down in the 1890s.

Lasha, seen here near the turn of the century, looked after the Hautier children during their long walk from Yale in 1860. Originally from a coastal tribe, Lasha remained with the Hautier family for many years. Note the home-made kiddie car on the right.

In the 1860s any cluster of buildings along the trail was a welcome sight. Top left, the earliest preserved photo of Lytton depicts both the original Globe Hotel and its stables on the opposite side of the street.

One feature of the Globe was its "homebrew." At Lytton, where the climate is warm and dry, the Hautier family grew grapes on their farm and produced several varieties of wine for use in their hotel saloon. After their parents retired to the farm, Albert Hautier, Fred McNeill, and Alphonse Hautier (top right) were the hotel's hosts. The door to the right led to the detention room, where rowdies were kept until they sobered up. The Globe remained the main watering hole for the men of the area. Below, the hotel chairs and patrons have been moved outdoors for this group photo.

The outward appearance of the Globe Hotel changed several times during the Hautier family's 40-year tenure. The fancy false front (above left), with a second floor and balcony, followed the arrival of the CPR in the late 1880s. After selling the hotel in 1896 to Samuel Adler, the Hautier brothers stayed on to manage the Globe for the next four years.

Lytton was plagued with fires during the 1930s and 1940s, when most of the important buildings on Main Street were destroyed, not just once, but, in some cases, twice. The last Globe Hotel (above right), a two-storey structure, was destroyed by fire in 1937.

Another Early Hotel

The original Lytton Hotel was built in the late 1860s opposite the Globe Hotel and next to the Globe Stable. Shown with an ox team at rest on Main Street, this hotel was originally built by William McWha and was taken over by George Baillie sometime after 1872. An Overlander of 1862 and originally from Edinburgh, Scotland, Baillie (left) played a violin in the dance halls of Barkerville prior to his move to Lytton. The Overlanders came in several groups in 1862 from what is now Ontario. They travelled across Canada to reach the gold rush in the Cariboo. Arriving at Quesnel in October, they were too late for that year and had to travel on to the lower mainland for the winter. Many of them returned the following spring. Following Baillie's death in 1887 the hotel changed hands twice before 1912, when the structure was razed by new owner, Hugh McGuire, to make way for a 60-room hotel.

This new three-storey structure survived fewer than twenty years. When fire destroyed McGuire's Lytton Hotel (shown below) and most of the business section of the town in 1931, another hotel, the New Lytton Hotel, was built by Antonio Medori.

Graveyards of the Fraser Canyon

In addition to his hotel property on Lot 5, Block 11, of Lytton town, Louis Hautier pre-empted 30 acres of arable land two miles south in May of 1861. Here the Hautiers grew vegetables to supply the needs of their hotel kitchen.

Upon the death of their three-year-old son William in 1869, the Hautiers established a family graveyard on this pre-emption. Today there are five graves within the enclosure, including William, Louis's wife (Josephine Dubois Vanderbrook, who died on September 13, 1881, at age 44), and Louis (January 3, 1886). Two other graves, which are slabbed over, remain unidentified. This registered graveyard is now part of the land owned by the Lytton Lumber Company, which is bound under an agreement with the town not to disturb this historic site, cared for by Lytton's cemetery committee.

The Hautier graveyard is enclosed by cement posts and heavy wire, as is seen in this picture taken in 1986.

Photographer Frederick Dally used his camera to document a changing world as he trekked to the Cariboo in 1867. Near Lytton, this chief's grave ignored the teaching of the missionaries. With time, however, the local Natives adopted new ways, as is evident in the Native graveyard (below) between Boston Bar and Lytton.

Lytton to Lillooet

While more popularly known for his enormous finds of gold on lower Williams Creek (Cameronton) in 1862, John A. (Cariboo) Cameron and his associates had even earlier successes on a rich gold bar ten miles north of Lytton in 1859. Within sight of the diggings was a large log roadhouse that served not only Cameron's men but also an increasing number of travellers to the Interior. The house was said to be scrupulously clean; it had a clay-roofed bake oven outside the door.

By 1860 Cameron Bar had become the site of a roadhouse farm operated by two Mexicans, Antonio Guerrera and Jose Tressierra. Bishop Hills and his party ate dinner here on their return from Lillooet that year. The two Mexicans remained at Cameron Bar for many years, pre-empting 360 acres in 1869.

In this 1863 photo (left), John A "Cariboo" Cameron (seated, with the long beard), Robert Stevenson on his right, and three unknowns wear the look of their rich discoveries on Williams Creek in 1862.

Below is Foster's Bar, upstream from Cameron's Bar, one of the largest and richest on the river, where hundreds of miners worked during the 1860s and where Jack Foster, a miner from Whatcom County, kept a roadhouse.

Watkinson's 24 Mile House, Foster's Bar

Midway along the historic road between Lytton and Lillooet two historic roadhouses served travellers for over seven decades. Frederick Joseph Watkinson, originally of Redruth in Cornwall, England, kept a roadhouse for many years on his farm at Foster's Bar Creek, the 24 milepost on the road between Lytton and Lillooet. When Watkinson, his wife Catherine (Harris), and two small children first settled on this arable piece of Fraser River bench land in 1865, they lived in a tent while a permanent log house was being built. By 1866 the stagecoach was bringing travellers to enjoy the hospitality of the large two-storey log house. The six-bedroom house accommodated the eleven Watkinson children, and there were two extra rooms for guests. When this house burned down in 1912, Joseph Watkinson built a second home, this one of lumber, just prior to his death in 1914. This house is still standing on the farm, where a fourth generation of the Watkinson family resides and continues to work the land. An original barn, from before the turn of the century, still stands on the Watkinson property (upper left). The inset photo shows the Watkinson family beside the original log house.

When Watkinson's roadhouse burned down in 1913, Halfway House (below) was built at the 25 milepost on the road to Lillooet. Originally pre-empted in 1862 by John Roberts, the farm was sold in the early 1900s to Archibald McGillivray. During the 1940s his son Charles sold the property to the Buckerfield Seed Company. In December of 1948 the home was destroyed in a fire caused by an overheated stovepipe.

Lillooet

An instant gold-rush town of 1859, Lillooet literally exploded to accommodate the miners who had come north from the lower Fraser River. Seen above in Charles Gentile's 1865 photo and below right in local merchant Archie Phair's 1920s photo is Lillooet's wide main street — wide enough, it was said, to turn a span of oxen. While Herkimer's Stage Hotel was the pioneer hostelry in Lillooet in 1859, the International, built by Spelman and McKenzie in 1866, was followed by several others. The Pioneer, built in the 1860s by Charles Nelson, became the Excelsior in the early 1900s and burned down shortly after this Phair photo was taken.

A later establishment, the Victoria Hotel (seen bottom left), was built in 1892 by Dan Hurley, for many years an entrepreneur and leading Lillooet-area businessman. The Victoria Hotel burned down in 1981. The upper inset photo shows the Mile 0 cairn, the point from which many roadhouses along the trails north derived their mileage and names.

Fort Berens and Parsonsville

The story of Fort Berens is the story of the fort that never was. In late 1858 the HBC applied for property on which to locate a post on the east bank of the Fraser River across from Cayoosh Creek. In 1859, when the HBC submitted a tabular statement of claim, the area in question covered 50 acres. Named for H.H. Berens, both a governor and a deputy governor of the HBC, the post was never built.

By 1861 the abandoned site of Fort Berens had become a supply depot for pack trains destined for the Cariboo goldfields. As it grew, the area became known as Parsonsville, after Otis Parsons (left), a packer and foreman involved in the building of the Port Douglas-to-Lillooet trail in 1858.

Alexander Kennedy pre-empted the site of Parsonsville in 1863 and within two years had acquired 620 acres, which he sold to Jonathan Scott, an American entrepreneur from New York. Scott was known to have grown and processed the first tobacco crops in the interior of British Columbia, most of which were sold to the miners. Scott spent the rest of his life in the Lillooet area. A brass plaque dedicated to Jonathan Scott was placed upon his grave, close to the original tobacco press, by MLA George Murray in 1958. Margaret "Ma" Murray, George's wife, was an acclaimed newspaper publisher and an avid historian. She always took time in her busy routine to watch over the various historic sites in the Lillooet area.

The Trail North

In the early 1860s traffic over the pack trails north of Lillooet and Parsonsville grew steadily. While pressure increased to complete a wagon road through the Fraser Canyon, strings of mules, horses, and even camels continued to haul supplies to the trail blazers. Just as the early gold seekers had followed the Fraser River

north of Lillooet, so did the packers. Ahead lay the challenge of Rattlesnake Hill and the ascent of Pavilion Mountain. Once there, the pack trains could look forward to a relatively inviting march across the rolling hill country and rangeland that carried all the way to Williams Lake.

Margaret "Ma" Murray, veteran newspaperwoman of Lillooet, beside Scott's grave in May of 1976.

The brass plaque dedicated to the pioneer Jonathan Scott.

Parsonsville to Pavilion Mountain

Gustavus Blin Wright, who built most of the Cariboo Wagon Road between 1862 and 1865, would ironically turn to running a riverboat.

Gustavus B. Wright and His Road

Spring of 1862 saw the start of road building in the interior of British Columbia. From Yale to Lytton an eighteen-foot-wide wagon road was built by contractors Thomas Spence and Joseph Trutch, and from Nicomen to Clinton the contract was awarded to Charles Oppenheimer and Walter Moberly. While Spence and Trutch completed their contracts in good time, Moberly and Oppenheimer ran into problems keeping enough men on the job. Not only were men leaving to join the gold rush, but later crews of Chinese and Native labourers died from an epidemic of smallpox.

At the same time Gustavus Blin Wright received a contract to build a second road from Lillooet to Clinton, an extension of the 1858 Port Douglas-to-Lillooet trail. Commencing in March at Parsonsville across the Fraser River from Lillooet, Wright assembled 250 men to work on the project.

Sergeant John McMurphy, RE

Road-building contracts of the time required the presence of a representative of the Royal Engineers to oversee the project and to measure the road as it was built. Sergeant John McMurphy, a veteran of the Crimean War and an experienced engineer, was assigned to G.B. Wright's project. As Wright won further contracts, McMurphy remained with the work crews until the road reached Alexandria in August of 1863.

During over one and a half years of road building, Sergeant McMurphy's daily log described the progress of the road builders and the traffic going by and provided information on many of the roadhouses he encountered.

Wright's road ran 22 miles from Parsonsville to Pavilion Creek. There he built a bridge and a nine-mile stretch of switchbacks to reach a plateau on Pavilion Mountain. Just why Wright chose to take his road over the precipitous Pavilion Mountain trail has never been resolved. As Wright was always strapped for money, it is thought that he may have been financially compensated for building the road past the several ranches in that remote area.

Haskell's 29 Mile House and a community of co-op farmers were already settled on the plateau when Wright's road reached it. The site was abandoned after the Fraser Canyon route was opened.

While there had been earlier settlers at the top of Pavilion Mountain, Robert Carson, who arrived in 1867, became the first permanent resident. With the stagecoach going by his door, it was not long before Carson was accommodating travellers at his log cabin (see page 27). In the late 1870s Robert married Eliza Jane Magee of Fraser Arm, and the Carsons raised ten children.

Sergeant and Mrs. John McMurphy. McMurphy's diary, kept during the building of the wagon road between Lillooet and Alexandria (1862-63), is one of the few to have survived to give us a glimpse of conditions and developments in the Cariboo.

The Fraser River above Lillooet, with the Fountain Ranch in the background.

The Fountain and Fountain House

An area known as the Fountain, eight miles northeast of Lillooet, became an important supply centre for miners in 1858. Situated on a high, grassy terrace above the Fraser River, it was named by French Canadians for the natural springs that came bubbling up out of the ground, turning the semi-arid terraces into an oasis of highly productive land.

In view of these natural advantages an Italian, Lorenzo Latora, was the first to pre-empt land in the area, where he started a farm and opened a roadhouse. Latora imported grape cuttings from Italy and sponsored three of his countrymen to establish his vineyard. The grapes made a delicious wine, which was served at the roadhouse. Dried grapes (raisins) were purchased by the miners to take with them on the trail. Latora remained at the Fountain until his death in 1888. His obituary in Victoria's *Colonist* read: "Owner of one of the finest farms in the region, his hospitality was unbounded." The site of Latora's farm is now Native reserve land.

The pen-and-ink drawing below, produced for the London Illustrated News *in 1859, depicts miners departing from Latora's roadhouse at the Fountain, close to their bench claims at Bridge River and Lillooet, where rich gold deposits had been found. By the spring of 1860 miners were travelling north again on the Fraser River and overland to the Cariboo.*

The 22 Mile House

Seen above is the site of one of the earliest roadhouse farms in the interior of British Columbia. Located 22 miles from Lillooet, on the Marble Canyon Road, it was approximately two miles east of the point where the road crossed Pavilion Creek. First inhabited in 1858 by David Reynolds, a squatter, the land was pre-empted in 1861 by Captain John Martley and sold in the late 1890s to John B. Bryson and his partner John C. Smith. The photo above (taken around 1912) shows the lodge, which was started in the 1880s by John's son Arthur Martley (inset) and completed by John Bryson. It burned down in 1949.

From the bridge across Pavilion Creek the road begins its sharp nine-mile ascent, by way of several switchbacks, up the side of the mountain. At the top is a large plateau of land where there has always been a trail of sorts, and while it is safe enough in summer, it is a treacherous place in winter.

The sketch (left) from Cheadle's book is of Rattlesnake Grade on 4,000-foot-high Pavilion Mountain. Below is seen part of the mountain as it slopes towards the Fraser River.

Pavilion Mountain

The Carson homestead (below right) atop Pavilion plateau proved fertile ground for Robert Carson and Eliza Jane Magee (above right), who were married in the late 1870s. They raised ten children, all of them well educated, and two of their sons became representatives of Lillooet and Kamloops in the provincial legislature.

Above, about 1900, members of the family pose outside their log cabin roadhouse. From left to right (back row) are Ella, Robert Carson, George, Fred, and Robert Carson Jr. From left to right (front row) are: Minnie, Edith, Mrs. Eliza Jane, and Edna. The top-right photo is of Eliza Jane Carson at the log-house door.

Below left is the modern house built by J. Edward (Ted) Termuende, a later owner of the Carson property. The new house was built around Carson's log house. In May of 1987, when this photo was taken, Mr. Termuende was found working along one wall of his living room to expose the logs from Carson's house. The large squared logs, with wide layers of white mortar in between them, made for an impressive conversation piece.

From Pavilion Mountain, Wright's wagon road turned northeast to Clinton. During its heyday at least ten log roadhouses (from Martley's at 22 Mile to the Spanish Ranch just south of Clinton) were built, all offering varying degrees of accommodation.

Further Up the Fraser: The Pack Trail to Williams Lake

While the majority of the 30,000 miners in British Columbia in 1858 remained to work in and near Lillooet, by spring of the following year, as a result of the findings of miner Aaron Post, various groups started up the Fraser River. Post had found gold 90 miles north of Lillooet at the mouth of the Chilcotin River, and from there the race to find the source of the Fraser gold gathered

momentum. At first the river afforded the only access into the vast wilderness of the northern Interior, for until the building of overland routes from Lillooet there were only Native trails and the HBC brigade routes from Fort Kamloops and Fort St. James.

From Lillooet to Alkali Lake, mining camps sprang up on both sides of the river. Following the arrival of overland mule trains in 1860, there were no fewer than seven trading posts and at least half a dozen roadhouses in the area.

Mountain House, Jesmond, BC

Near Big Bar Creek, 60 miles north of Lillooet, Philip Grinder, an 1858 miner, ran a ranch and roadhouse known as the Mountain House. By 1914 Harry G. Coldwell and his wife Louise had taken over the Mountain House Ranch, where they accommodated guests travelling on the overland stagecoach route between Clinton and Dog Creek. The local post office became known as Jesmond.

Seen on the upper left is the original Mountain House built by Philip Grinder, and below is the present house, built in 1922 by Harry Coldwell.

Dog Creek

Predating the gold rush, a Mexican packer, Raphael Valenzuela, built a winter cabin at Dog Creek that became part of a roadhouse operated by the Joseph Smith Place family in the 1880s. At one time there were five separate hotels, each with its own saloon, operating in Dog Creek. Settlers were growing enough grain to supply what became the first flour mill on the BC mainland. Chinese miners who continued to work their claims along the Fraser supported the local economy. By the early 1900s the miners were gone, and some of the smaller ranches started to disappear.

During the depression of the 1930s a second generation of the Place family struggled to regain the ranch after it was foreclosed upon, as a result of Joseph Smith's loans. It took the ingenuity and strength of Ada Place to accomplish this.

Left is Dog Creek House in 1912, and above is a barn originally built in the early 1900s.

Alkali Lake

Just downstream from the mouth of the Chilcotin River and seventeen miles north of Dog Creek, in 1859 Herman O. Bowe had a trading post and roadhouse at Cardis Bar. By 1861 he and his partner Philip Grinder had pre-empted land at the head of Alkali Lake. The Alkali Lake Ranch has changed hands many times but remains one of the largest ranches in the region.

To the right is a sample of an 1861 application to pre-empt land in the Lillooet land recording area. In this case, Herman Bowe and his partner travelled (probably on horseback) to Lillooet, a journey of several days, where their claims were registered by Magistrate Thomas Elwyn.

Below are seen the buildings of Alkali Lake Ranch circa 1920, with the original log cabin roadhouse in the mid-foreground. Today this is considered to be one of the most valuable ranches in the Interior.

Thomas Elwyn (left inset) remained in government service for many years, as a magistrate and government agent at Richfield in 1862, and as deputy provincial secretary during the A.C. Elliot government of the 1870s.

No of record
15

Certificate of improvement issed to H.O. Bowe by Mr. Elmyn this 4th Dec. 1862.

Recorded this 19th day of March 1861 in favour of H. O. Bowe & Philip Grinder the preemption-right to three hundred and twenty (320) acres of land situated at the head of Alkali lake & running north west from the creek as shown in this accompanying sketch.

(Signed) Thomas Elwyn J.P.

Springhouse

Springhouse was so named for St. Peter's Spring, where Father Demers visited the Native people in the 1840s and where they erected a cross in his remembrance. Located in a wide, prairie-like valley between Alkali Lake and Williams Lake, Springhouse was on the original fur-trader pack trail.

The land at Springhouse, about 20 miles northeast of Alkali Lake, has been cultivated since 1862, when a Cornish farmer, with two partners, operated a farm and roadhouse. An Italian packer, Augustine Boitanio, purchased the ranch in 1885 and lived there with his large family for many years. Boitanio, who for years had packed for the HBC between Fort Langley and Fort St. James, had often passed through the wide, pleasantly situated valley on the original pack trail. In 1901 young Arthur Crease, the son of Judge Henry Crease and a friend of Joe Pemberton, bicycled up from the Coast to Springhouse on a holiday. Crease, a disciplined diarist, was most impressed with the musical talents of the family and with the expert needlework of the girls. Seen below is a 1920s photo of Boitanio's roadhouse at Springhouse. In front is a group of young riders from the local area, including Alfie Eagle, who is enjoying his first ride.

The Boitanio Barn and Blacksmith Shop

An old story associated with Augustine Boitanio tells of a time when he had a pack train of 50 horses, mules, and donkeys. On one occasion, when a jackass got sick on the trail to the goldfields, Augustine left the animal to die at Springhouse Ranch. On his return the next spring, he was surprised to find the donkey alive and well. The animal lived for many years and was known to have sired 500 mules. The original barn on the Boitanio farm had been built of large fir logs cut on the property. It has survived through the years and is still in use.

While serving a different purpose now, in the days when horses were used for transportation, the blacksmith shop was one of the most important buildings on a farm or homestead, where metal wagon parts were forged and harness was repaired.

Chimney Creek

The origin of the name "Chimney Creek," an area ten miles south of Williams Lake, comes from a stone chimney — all that was left of a cabin built by the Shuswap for an early missionary, Father Demers, when he visited there in 1842. This must also have been the site of a Native village, for today the remains of pit houses are seen near the creek.

The Chimney Creek Ranch is one of the most historic in the Cariboo. Pre-empted in 1861 by John Laveau, a French voyageur, the land was then transferred to John Rose. By 1876 the ranch had fallen to Amadee Isnardy. This French adventurer from Nice, and his wife Julienne Willamatkwa, added many more acres to the ranch.

This house was built by William Bowe of Alkali Lake.

The original roadhouse (above) was built in the late 1860s. Containing five bedrooms upstairs and an accommodating kitchen and bar room on the main floor, it was a popular meeting place for packers and miners at a time when heavy traffic was passing by on the river trail from Lillooet. Amadee and Julienne had a large family, the descendants of whom still live in the region.

The Chimney and Felker Lakes area has also been home to members of the second generation of the pioneer Felker family. Patrick, third son of Henry and Antonette Felker of 127 Mile and 144 Mile on the Cariboo Road, took up land at Chimney Lake in 1877, where he built a log home near the lake named for him.

The two-storey log building pictured on the right is known as the Haunted House. Built on land originally owned by H.O. Bowe of Alkali Lake, it was sold to the Felker brothers in the late 1890s. According to the story, the building was once a roadhouse in which an overnight stopper died under suspicious circumstances. While the roadhouse proprietor attempted to hush the story up, the ghost of the deceased visited the roadhouse guests at night and scared them all away.

This 1968 photo shows a second abandoned structure on the property originally owned by the Felker family.

Williams Lake: The Early Years

Due to its modern-day prominence, there is a common misconception that the community of Williams Lake grew up beside the Cariboo Wagon Road. In fact the original homesteads were on the older pack-train route from Lillooet. In 1863 the wagon road bypassed Williams Lake, and the area remained a backwater until the arrival of the Pacific Great Eastern (PGE) Railway in 1919.

Known as Columneetza, an area inhabited by the Shuswap for thousands of years, the site of Williams Lake was pre-empted in 1860 by an American miner, Thomas Davidson. Within a year Davidson's farm and roadhouse had become an important jumping-off place for miners on the upper Fraser, Horsefly, and Quesnel Rivers. By fall of 1861 Davidson had sold his farm to Thomas Menefee, one of Peter Dunlevy's mining partners.

In the meantime a second roadhouse farm, operated by William Pinchbeck (a policeman) and his partners Thomas Meldrum and William Lyne, had commenced operations at Williams Lake. The consortium became known as Pinchbeck and Company. When Thomas Meldrum left the area in 1866 to start a ranch of his own on the west side of the Fraser River, he sold his share in the property back to Pinchbeck.

The two roadhouse farms at Williams Lake continued operating until the 1870s, when Menefee died and Pinchbeck and Lyne became the principal landowners in the area, having control over 1,000 acres of ranchland.

Below is the Lake House, Pinchbeck's 1886 residence situated at the foot of Williams Lake. In later years, following the sale of the ranch to the PGE, Lake House became a boarding house for men working on railway construction.

William Lyne Sr. (middle), Thomas Meldrum and his wife (left), and William Pinchbeck and his wife Alice Kilham Pinchbeck (right).

The original buildings (c. 1868) on the Pinchbeck property were known as the Lower House.

The Pinchbeck farm produced large crops of grain, some of which was made into flour in a grist mill on the property and some of which was processed into liquor to sell to the mining camps. While Lyne dissolved his partnership in 1888 and moved to Ashcroft, Pinchbeck remained on the farm until his death in 1893. Taken at the time of William Pinchbeck's death, this photo

(right) shows those paying their respects: (from the right) Annie Anders, Angelique (Dussault) Lyne, Mary Collingsworth Lyne, and William Lyne Sr. At the time of his death, his wife Alice and their two sons were in England.

The Pinchbeck family's connection with Williams Lake had an unfortunate end. When 62-year-old William died he owed a substantial debt to the operators of the nearby Gang Ranch and was behind in his obligations. By the time Alice Pinchbeck returned to their home after her husband's death, all the furniture and equipment had been auctioned off in order to satisfy William's debts. Unable to find a buyer, the Gang Ranch leased the Pinchbeck property to Joseph Patenaude and his sons Albert and Ernest.

The Arrival of the Wagon Road

One of the true legacies of the gold rush was that it led to a broad spectrum of adventurers settling in the Cariboo. Many pioneer families trace their roots to ancestors who pre-empted land through which packers made the first trails and even more connect their heritage to the building of the Cariboo Wagon Road.

While following the pack trains we have reached well into the Cariboo and arrived at Williams Lake. Before continuing north, this is an appropriate juncture at which to leave the pack trail and return south to continue the saga of wagon road construction beyond Lytton at the confluence of the Fraser and Thompson Rivers. Royal Engineers had determined that the building of a road through the Thompson Canyon as an extension of the earlier conquest of the Fraser Canyon was the ultimate route to the Cariboo. Gold seekers, merchants, and settlers alike would be able to reach their destinations with great expedience and comfort.

By 1863, a year behind schedule, east and north from where the Thompson River joins the mighty Fraser, the ultimate wagon road was slowly making headway. It was a route that would, for the next century, dictate much of the flow of traffic into British Columbia's interior.

Carving Through the Thompson Canyon and Heading North to Clinton

While the original pack trail through Dog Creek and the Springhouse Valley retained some traffic, 1862 would change traffic patterns to the Cariboo forever. Clinton was already the terminus of G.B. Wright's first road contract from Lillooet east. But the real boom lay ahead, as determined contractors undertook to build a wagon road through the great river canyons of the Fraser and Thompson. Initially the route from Lytton had followed the Fraser north to Lillooet, where it merged with the Port Douglas-to-Lillooet trail.

Engineers had charted a more favourable route beside the Thompson that would expedite the movement of cargo to and from the goldfields. That route would hug the southeast wall of the canyon from Lytton to Cook's Ferry, then parallel the western bank of the Thompson River before turning to where Cache Creek meets the Bonaparte River.

The building of the Cariboo Wagon Road through the Fraser and Thompson Canyons was one of the great achievements of nineteenth-century North American road building. Photographer Frederick Dally captured the dramatic setting of the Great Bluff during his 1867 journey to the Cariboo (above). There is little doubt that Dally's photo helped to inspire G.A. Cuthbertson's rendering, over 70 years later, in the October 1935 Canadian Mining Journal.

Labour Problems

In March of 1862 tenders were put out for the building of the road from Lytton to Clinton, which was to be completed by July 15 of that year. The successful bidder was the firm of Oppenheimer, Moberly and Lewis, composed of Charles Oppenheimer, head of the great mercantile firm of Oppenheimer Brothers; Walter Moberly, a well-known civil engineer; and T.B. Lewis, an associate of Oppenheimer.

With the help of a very large crew, the work proceeded well for a time, and by June twelve miles of road had been completed past Nicomen. Unfortunately for the contractor, wild rumours of the riches of the Cariboo began to circulate, and many of the crew defected. Fewer than two years later, with local gold mined out, the population of Nicomen dispersed. In 1864 Barnard's stagecoach didn't even stop here.

Given the mass exodus of the wagon road work crew, the government extended the contract to August 16. Replacements, primarily local Natives, were hired and worked well until they were decimated by an outbreak of smallpox. Without sufficient crew to undertake the work, and with the road almost half built, the contractors were forced to forfeit on their agreement with the government. In October 1863 a new contract was awarded to William Hood of Santa Clara, California, to build the road from the "big rock bluff" above Cook's Ferry (Spences Bridge) to Clinton.

Nicomen

One curiosity of the 1862 Cariboo Wagon Road is that it was built to include Nicomen, twelve miles east of Lytton. This was due to the fact that during the early 1860s Nicomen, on the Thompson River, included a population of prospectors and miners that was generating large amounts of commerce and freight. There had been a roadhouse in the community of Nicomen since the start of the gold rush, and it would see a second heyday. During the 1870s, when optimism over the proposed route of the CPR ran high, Nicomen House, the store and roadhouse (top middle) was owned by John Clapperton (inset), a tax collector at Spences Bridge.

The members of this congregation outside the 80 Mile House at Cook's Ferry (top left), photographed when Frederick Dally passed their way in 1867, seem content to listen to the resident cook play his fiddle. John Clapperton (upper right), owner of Nicomen House in the 1870s.

A significant step in upgrading the new road was to replace Mortimer Cook's ferry with Thomas Spence's bridge in 1865 (left).

Where there were no roadhouses, packers would make camp along their route. Photographer Charles Gentile passed by this pack train at an unnamed camp in the Thompson Canyon in 1865.

The Basque Ranch

Bordering the Thompson River at the 97 milepost (from Yale), seventeen miles north of Spences Bridge, the Basque Ranch has a fascinating history that dates back to 1861, when a group of Basque farmers emigrated from Oregon with a herd of cattle.

Operated for many years by Louis Antoine Minnaberriet, the son of a French aristocrat from the Basque area, the cattle and mixed-farming operation was eventually consolidated into one ranch, which included a successful roadhouse and stagecoach stop for the BC Express Company. The Minnaberriets were resourceful. At one time, while strapped for cash, Minnaberriet and his sons set up their sluice boxes along the edge of the Thompson River below their ranch and managed to recover $70,000 in gold.

In speculation of the 1883 arrival of the CPR, Minnaberriet sold the ranch to two Englishmen — the Langley brothers. They paid $40,000 for the property, which included full water rights. A large part of the bottomland of the Basque Ranch was at this time leased to Chinese farmers, who, upon the arrival of the railway, began living in the area. The Chinese grew large crops of tomatoes, which, in the early 1900s, they sold to the canneries near Ashcroft. By 1930 the ranch had been sold to the Marston family and, still later, it was sold to Skelton and Stoddard before becoming a part of the Cook's Ferry Indian Reserve.

The Basque Ranch abounds in legends and stories, one of which concerns a hidden gold cache left by a miner who murdered his partner, and several others concerning robberies.

The roadhouse (above right) on the Basque Ranch as it was during the 1980s.

The remains of log cabins built by the Chinese in the early 1900s (lower right).

Cornwall's Ashcroft Manor

Built of logs and whipsawn lumber in 1863, the Cornwall brothers' "Public," as they referred to their roadhouse, was at first a single-storey building measuring 20 feet by 40 feet. Ashcroft Manor continued as a roadhouse until the 1960s, making it one of the few to reach 100 years of operation.

It was not until the early 1900s — when Clement Cornwall's married daughter Caroline, her husband George Barclay, and their four children went to live at the manor — that a second storey was added to the roadhouse. This almost doubled its capacity, making room for several guest bedrooms. Unfortunately, Caroline Barclay suffered an agonizing death when bitten by a rattlesnake. The last of the Cornwall family to live at Ashcroft Manor was Vashti Parker Fisk, her husband T.C. (Trav), and her four children.

Today the restored manor is a visitor's delight, not only for its historical significance, but also for its showroom displaying beautiful gifts and local crafts.

Charles Gentile took this photo (below) while visiting the Cornwall's "Ashcroft" in 1865, two years after the original cabin roadhouse was completed. Two photos (right) show an active roadhouse in the 1880s and the original one-storey structure. The manor was restored shortly after this photo (upper right) was taken in the 1980s.

The Butte Ranch and the Beginnings of Ashcroft

A flat river bench on the southeast bank of the Thompson River inadvertently became the site of the new town of Ashcroft in the mid-1880s. Known as the Butte Ranch, a property previously overlooked by pre-emptors due to its remote location, several hundred acres were taken up in the late 1860s by two American adventurers — John C. Barnes and his partner William Brink. This is where they lived, raised their families, and shared the work.

As construction of the CPR moved west in 1883, it became apparent that a northwest station point would be established on the east bank of the Thompson River, and the Butte Ranch was the logical location. While Billy Brink did not live to reap the financial benefits of his suddenly prime property, his partner Barnes and his son-in-law Oliver Evans did. As the first train chugged up the track, Barnes and Evans were busy surveying and selling town lots.

Oliver Evans (above), a founding father of Ashcroft.

To the left, William Lyne Sr., owner of the Ashcroft Hotel in 1890, and his wife Mary Collingsworth, a former Wisconsin belle who first settled in Ashcroft with her new husband in 1887.

Below, a team of ten and three wagons take a break at the top of Ashcroft Hill, heading north.

The Ashcroft Hotel

In 1886 a large new hotel, the Ashcroft, built by Oliver Evans and his partner E.E. Bligh, appeared across the street from the railway station. By the 1890s Evans had sold his interest in the hotel to Bligh, who took on a new partner, William Lyne Sr., a former associate of William Pinchbeck of Williams Lake. By 1898 Lyne had become owner of the hotel, where he continued on until his untimely death in 1903.

In the upper picture is seen the well-appointed saloon of the Ashcroft Hotel, where men stood shoulder to shoulder every evening, except on Sunday. The lobby of the hotel had a large, black-and-white checkerboard floor covering, and within sight of the front door was a noisy, multicoloured African parrot who lived in a large cage. The parrot, which was there from the 1940s, had mastered a large vocabulary, including many swear words, which it used to gain attention when visitors entered the hotel. It is not known whether the bird was rescued when the hotel burned down in 1974.

Below is the Ashcroft Hotel, the most popular hotel in the town between 1886 and 1974.

The Cariboo Wagon Road: Cache Creek and Clinton

Cache Creek/Bonaparte House

In 1862 James Orr (bottom left) built Bonaparte House atop Rattlesnake Hill, but after three winters he sold the building to Charles Semlin (middle). Semlin, who would become the premier of British Columbia in 1898, and his partner, Philip Parke (right), moved Bonaparte House to the bottom of the hill, enlarged it, and commenced operations. In 1868 Parke sold his interest to William Sanford and left to start his own ranch at Cache Creek. There, five years later, when the government authorized the building of the Cache Creek Boarding School, Philip Parke donated the land.

The top photo, the earliest known picture of Cache Creek (c. 1866), shows Bonaparte House and the farm at the bottom of Rattlesnake Hill. The two tandem freight wagons no doubt stopped at the roadhouse. After 1868, when the house was operated by William "Boston" Sanford (see two photos, left), the original "Bonaparte" sign was changed to "Cache Creek House, Boston." After 1870 William Sanford went on to new adventures, and any reference to Boston went with him.

The 12 Mile House North of Ashcroft

Following the arrival of the CPR and the rise of the town of Ashcroft in the mid-1880s, the government of the day attempted to institute new mileage signs along the wagon road, starting from Ashcroft. These were to replace the older signs, which started from Lillooet and Yale, respectively. The new system failed, with only one or two roadhouses willing to adapt to the change.

The 12 Mile House (north of Ashcroft) was established in 1893 by Cole McDonald and his wife, the former Rose Veasy. Located beside the original wagon road, which at that time skirted the west side of the Bonaparte Valley, the roadhouse was situated on a small homestead south of the Hat Creek Ranch. For twelve years the McDonalds, with the help of their ten children, operated a very popular roadhouse, store, saloon, and blacksmith shop, catering mostly to freighters and the stagecoach.

A school was built nearby to provide education for the large McDonald family and the several Robertson children from Upper Hat Creek. When one of the children forgot to take his or her lunch to school, which happened occasionally, he or she had only to walk over to the roadhouse, where Mrs. McDonald would take care of matters.

In 1914, following the death of Cole McDonald, Rose sold out and moved her family to Victoria. The property is now part of the Hat Creek Ranch.

First two scenes above are of the 12 Mile House in 1915. The BC Express stagecoach is seen leaving for the north. Aboard is said to be Captain O.F. Browne, master of the steamship BX.

The lower picture shows that the roadhouse had been extended to include a saloon entrance. Access to the lobby was through the garden and under the porch.

Hat Creek House

Purchased by the British Columbia Heritage Trust in 1981, Hat Creek House and Ranch has a long and varied history that dates back to the fur-trade era of 1842, when HBC employees at Fort Kamloops used the area as a wintering ground for their horses. When Donald McLean retired as chief trader at Fort Kamloops in 1860, he and his large family settled in the Bonaparte Valley near the confluence of Hat Creek and the Bonaparte River. With a growing population of miners passing through the region on their way to and from the Cariboo goldfields, McLean's Station, as it was first known, became a popular stopping place. Donald McLean was killed in the Chilcotin War of 1864.

While the McLeans were the first to settle at Hat Creek, the first to pre-empt land at the mouth of Hat Creek (the site of Hat Creek House) was Neil McArthur, also a former HBC employee, who in 1861 transported some abandoned buildings to the site. These he made habitable for travellers on the gold-rush trail. Since then there have been many owners of Hat Creek House: George Dunne in 1866, Jerome Harper in 1876, William Cargile in 1881, Steven Tingley in 1887, Charles Doering in 1910, and Basil Jackson in 1927.

Following a period of restoration (initiated by the BC Heritage Trust) between 1981 and 1987, the 20-room roadhouse and surrounding grounds have been open to the public each summer between June and the end of September. On Heritage Day, a special event held at the end of June each year, visitors participate in a period-costume contest, enjoy old-fashioned races, and take in outdoor displays of home crafts, historical books, and art work.

Hat Creek House in the 1980s, before and after restoration by the BC Heritage Trust. Started as a small building in 1861, the structure has been enlarged through the years, with a west wing added in 1901. Containing 20 rooms, it is the largest of the original roadhouses still standing.

Hat Creek Ranch was an outstanding property (see photo below) when wealthy Vancouver businessman Charles Doering bought it in 1910. By the mid-1930s, a decade after Doering's death, Hat Creek Ranch was taken over by Doering's nephew Basil and his wife Dorothy (Parke) Jackson. While the couple lived in the old roadhouse (inset) for some time, a modern bungalow was built nearby, to which they retired in the 1940s. Following her husband's death, Mrs. Jackson sold the bulk of the property to BC Hydro in view of the burgeoning of the Upper Hat Creek Coal Development. While BC Hydro did not keep the property, Hat Creek Ranch was later sold to the Province of British Columbia and declared a heritage site in 1981. Seen below are three men connected with the history of Hat Creek House.

Donald McLean (left) was for many years the tyrannical HBC factor who reputedly hated Native people yet had two Native wives. Steven Tingley (centre) was working as a saddle maker in Lytton in 1864 when he was hired by Francis J. Barnard to drive one of the first stagecoaches from Yale to Soda Creek. By 1879 the long-term driver had become the owner of the BC Express Company. Charles Doering (right), former president of the British Columbia Breweries Limited, bought the Hat Creek Ranch and roadhouse as a retirement home, where he could raise purebred racehorses and Shorthorn cattle.

The 20 Mile House from Ashcroft

Seen above is the one remaining original building on the 20 Mile Ranch. Once used as a blacksmith shop, this log building is just inside a fence on the south side of the road.

An 1863 pre-emption in the Bonaparte Valley was sold in 1870 to Jacob Mundorf and his wife Catherine (Haupt), originally from Germany. The two had met in Barkerville in the early 1860s, where Jacob was a merchant and Catherine was a hurdy-gurdy girl. With their four children, the Mundorfs kept a roadhouse and small ranch beside the Cariboo Road for 40 or so years.

By the mid-1880s, with the coming of the CPR to Ashcroft, roadhouses north of here enjoyed a resurgence of business. At Mundorfs a new and larger two-storey roadhouse was built beside the wagon road, which at that time ran along the west side of the valley. During this period the roadhouse's saloon became a very public place, with freighters coming and going at all hours, but not so the parlour. Although it was

tastefully decorated with expensive rosewood furniture, thick rugs, and a cozy heater, according to an account written by Edward K. DeBeck (a clerk in the BC legislature during the 1920s), the room was seldom used.

In 1891, as an eight-year-old, Edward Debeck, who suffered from bronchitis, was taken to live for part of a year in the dry, sunny climate of the Mundorf Ranch. Apparently his mother had made a deal with the Mundorfs: if they kept Edward, then she would keep their daughter Charlotte at school in Victoria. When the DeBecks first arrived at the Mundorf roadhouse they were shown into the parlour, where Edward noticed the fine furniture. As it turned out, Edward, who ate in the roadhouse kitchen and slept in the barn, was kept busy from dawn to dusk performing ranch chores and never saw the inside of the parlour again.

When in 1895 the government attempted to change the mileage system along the road north of Ashcroft, the Mundorf Ranch was one of very few to comply, becoming the 20 Mile House from Ashcroft rather than the 124 Mile House from Yale.

Seen here are two pieces of fine rosewood furniture that were saved from the fire of 1942, which burned the roadhouse down.

Dougherty's Maiden Creek Ranch. Taken in 1920, this picture (left) shows the second roadhouse built at Maiden Creek Ranch (the 126 Mile House from Yale and the 23 Mile House from Ashcroft). Built in the 1880s, this house burned down in 1951 and was replaced by another, which is still occupied by the Dougherty family.

Clinton

When photographer Richard Maynard reached Clinton (above) in 1868 it was already a well-established community. Residents and ranchers (right) met daily in the Clinton Hotel or at the toll office to hear the latest news from both north and south. After the gold rush to the north subsided, Clinton remained a supply centre for the ranches of the region.

By the late 1880s, after the CPR established a station only miles south of Clinton, the town and points north enjoyed a resurgence of travellers. In 1892 Clinton was a vibrant community (see bottom photo).

If there is one single roadhouse that symbolizes the first century of Cariboo hospitality, it is the Clinton Hotel, which was built at the junction of G.B. Wright's road from Lillooet and the road from Yale. For years the large, eight-room log structure was one of the most successful hotels on the Cariboo Wagon Road. Opened in 1862 by the Watson brothers and their partner McKinnon, the hotel gained immediate popularity with miners and packers. The three men had been working as members of G.B. Wright's roadbuilding crew when they realized the potential for a hotel at the junction of the Yale and Lillooet roads.

A later owner, Joseph L. Smith, established the Clinton Ball, the first of which was held in the billiard room of the enlarged hotel. This annual event, which continued on even after the hotel burned down, grew to become a three-day affair at which dancing and drinking continued until daylight. Then, after a few hours of sleep, the participants would begin their merrymaking all over again.

This Frederick Dally photo (top) of Bill Bose's ox team in front of the Clinton Hotel in the 1860s is possibly the most popular of all visual depictions of the journey north along the Cariboo Wagon Road. By Christmas Day 1894, when the second photo was taken, new siding gave the hotel a more modern look.

Taken outside the Clinton Hotel in 1907, this picture (lower left) marks the arrival of what is thought to be the first car to travel up the Cariboo Wagon Road. It was reputedly owned by the Guggenheim Company of Bullion Mine, near Likely. The famous hotel (pictured below in the 1950s) burned to the ground in 1958 in a fire that killed three people.

A popular boarding house in Clinton at the turn of the century was the Palace Hotel. The building, which was erected in 1873 and is still standing, has had the "gingerbreading" removed from the front porch but is still easily recognizable by the unique "Riverboat" insignia on its eaves.

In 1984, when the above photo was taken, the entire building was very much intact, except for the absence of the front porch.

The Palace Hotel in 1909 (right), with a BX stagecoach (BC Express No. 20) in the foreground. It must have been a cut above the average, for most of the boarders were teachers and single government men.

Below, a group of 30 poses outside the Dominion Hotel at Clinton on Christmas Day 1893. Mr. and Mrs. Robert Walker, owners of the hotel, stand on the far right. Financed by a group of businessmen from Cache Creek, the hotel had actually been built there and was then moved to Clinton (which was thought to be a better location) in 1893. This hotel burned down in 1908.

Clinton to the Williams Lake Area

The Big House on Pollard's Ranch

When John Pollard died in 1901, he left his wife Kezia and seven children to carry on with the operation of a large ranch just north of Clinton. Kezia also operated a roadhouse for people who travelled on the road that, at one time, ran through the ranch. So well did Kezia prosper that by 1908 she was able to build a large, two-storey frame building. Known originally as the Big House, this building still stands and continues to operate as a guesthouse.

Seen left is a 1908 photo of Kezia Pollard and her family with ranch foreman Jack Arthur, taken on the occasion of Charles Pollard's twenty-first birthday.

Below is Kezia's roadhouse, which still stands on the ranch.

The lower photo shows several cabins that were built later, when the Big House became a guest ranch.

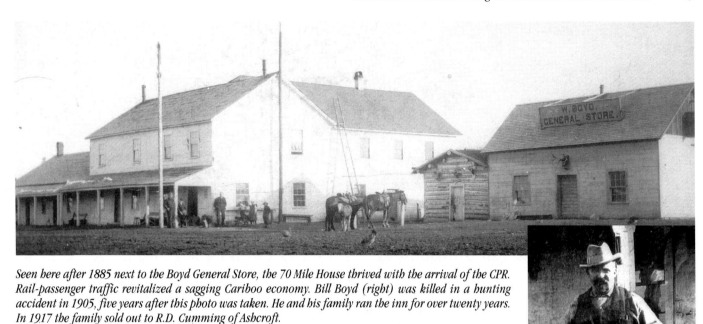

Seen here after 1885 next to the Boyd General Store, the 70 Mile House thrived with the arrival of the CPR. Rail-passenger traffic revitalized a sagging Cariboo economy. Bill Boyd (right) was killed in a hunting accident in 1905, five years after this photo was taken. He and his family ran the inn for over twenty years. In 1917 the family sold out to R.D. Cumming of Ashcroft.

The 70 Mile House

One of the most celebrated roadhouses on the Cariboo Wagon Road was the 70 Mile House. Started by G.B. Wright in 1862, the roadhouse changed hands often over the years, with many owners contributing to its development.

After taking over in 1875, the Saul brothers, William (left) and John, in anticipation of the arrival of the CPR in Ashcroft, added a whole wing and a second storey to the roadhouse, increasing its number of bedrooms to twelve. It was the Sauls who purchased the nearby Green Lake Meadows, where they pastured a herd of cows in order to provide dairy products to the roadhouse.

After 1885, the next owners, William Boyd and his family, reaped the benefits of the enlarged facility during a resurgence of traffic on the wagon road in the 1890s and early 1900s. The ones who owned the 70 Mile for the longest period were Matt and Isobel "Ma" Porter, who operated the landmark inn from 1920 until 1956, when it burned down.

Tourists pose at the 70 Mile House in the middle of the Cariboo Road in 1955, only a year before the heritage building was lost to fire.

The 74 Mile House

Sergeant John McMurphy of the Royal Engineers was the first to pre-empt land at the 74 milepost on the Cariboo Wagon Road in 1863. The venture proved unsuccessful, but 30 years later, in 1891, a young Scotsman named Jack Cunningham took up land at almost the same location. Jack soon married Margaret Clark of Edinburgh, and the couple raised a family of four children while operating a ranch and roadhouse at the 74 milepost. In 1910 Mrs. Cunningham lost her husband to pneumonia and her eldest son to a burst appendix. Despite her great loss, this brave woman worked resolutely to raise her children and to continue operating her popular roadhouse. The original house burned to the ground in 1923 but was replaced soon after. During the depression of the 1930s, the 74 Mile House became a dude ranch in the summer and a hostel for duck hunters in the fall. Assisted by her family, Margaret Clark Cunningham continued to operate her roadhouse until 1950, when a new road bypassed the 74 Mile House.

The original 74 Mile House (top), built in 1896. Above is Margaret Cunningham, who operated the 70 Mile House for almost six decades. This picture was taken in 1965, the year before she died.

The photo at the right is of the stagecoach and freighter leaving the 83 Mile House, circa 1870. Roadhouses were busy serving customers both day and night. "Move 'em out, we're burnin' daylight," was probably heard often along the road. After dinner, an hour's rest, and a change of horses, the travellers would continue up the Cariboo Road.

100 Mile House

A thriving community today, 100 Mile House was once a campground for HBC fur traders. It became a cattle ranch in 1859, when John and Oliver Jeffereys of Alabama arrived with a herd of 700 longhorn steers and cows. This area first became known as Bridge Creek when the Jeffereys built a toll bridge over the creek, but with the building of the wagon road from Lillooet, it became the 100 milepost. A roadhouse and store on the ranch thrived, and eventually there were five adjoining buildings. Through the years there were several owners of the 100 Mile House property — among them Mard Nelson, Charles Beak, Frank and Sydney Stevenson, and Thomas Hamilton.

In 1912 the ranch was sold to the Marquis of Exeter, but it was not until 1930 that Lord Martin Cecil came to British Columbia to take up residence — not in the old roadhouse, which was infested with bedbugs, but in a new lodge built especially for him. The old roadhouse burned down in 1937.

Seen here are John Jeffereys (top), who imported cattle and took up residence at 100 Mile in 1859; Thomas Hamilton (middle), who bought the ranch in 1880; and Lord Martin Cecil (bottom), who arrived to take possession of the property in 1930.

At the time of this 1900 photo (above), Frank and Sydney Stevenson owned 100 Mile House. The brothers ran a sawmill and a 3,000-acre spread until Sydney was killed in a hunting accident.

In 1868 the respected Victoria photographers Richard and Hannah Maynard stayed at the 100 Mile House. Here, Hannah and proprietor Mard Nelson are seen, with Richard behind the lens.

The 108 Mile Roadhouse and Ranch

William J. Roper, originally of Dorsetshire, England, was the first to pre-empt 160 acres of land at the 108 milepost on the wagon road from Lillooet. While freighting goods between Lillooet and the goldfields of Williams Creek in 1863, Roper passed through the area and was reminded of his home in England. Here he built a large, two-storey log roadhouse to accommodate the heavy traffic going by way of the 108 Mile trail to the Horsefly River, where rich deposits of gold were being discovered. Roper was not successful in his endeavours at the 108 Mile House, and in 1868, before returning to his former occupation as a freighter, he sold out to Charles M. Beak. It is not known when Roper's original roadhouse burned down, but later photos of the 108 Mile House, still standing today, show a very differently shaped building standing at approximately the same site. It may have been Beak who built this later structure.

Through the years the 108 Mile House Ranch had several owners. Among them were Charles Beck; William Walker and his wife Emily; Steven Tingley and his son Clarence; and, in the early 1900s, Captain Geoffrey L. Watson, an English Army officer who was killed in action during the First World War.

Seen here is William Roper (top inset) and his 1865 roadhouse. The small bottom photo shows the same house, with some improvements.

The 111 Mile House

First pre-empted in 1862 by a Mr. and Mrs. Cochrane, the 111 Mile Ranch and roadhouse changed hands several times over the years. A prime piece of real estate situated in a temperate climate and through which ran the wagon road, it was a natural site for a roadhouse during the gold-rush period.

By 1865 the Blair brothers, David and John, had built a large, two-storey frame hotel on the north side of the road, where travellers heading for the Horsefly and Quesnel Lake area remained overnight. After only a year, when business did not materialize, the property was sold to William Manson, a retired HBC trader. Manson settled at the 111 Mile House Ranch in order to accommodate his wife, a relative of the McKinlay family, who resided at the 115 Mile House. The Mansons moved again when Archibald and Sarah McKinlay retired to Savona. William Abel, the schoolteacher at Lac la Hache during the 1880s, remained in the area after the school closed for lack of pupils. In the meantime Abel bought the 111 Mile Ranch and, with his wife and several children, operated the 360-acre farm and roadhouse for several years. The 111 Mile roadhouse was at that time a regular BC Express stage stop on the road between Ashcroft and Barkerville. The stage pulled in for breakfast twice a week at 6:00 AM. When it seemed unlikely that a school would open at Lac la Hache, Abel moved his family to the coast.

Right is William Abel, schoolteacher at Lac la Hache in the 1880s and one-time owner of the 111 Mile Ranch and roadhouse.

In the photo taken by Gentile (left) are Lac la Hache neighbours William Manson of the 111 Mile House and Archibald McKinlay of the 115 Mile House.

When H.J. Boam and A.G. Brown's book British Columbia *was published in England in 1912, this photo presented the 111 Mile House as a tranquil frontier ranch.*

The 115 Mile Ranch and Roadhouse

The McKinlay, Ogden, Hamilton, and McDougall families, all one-time employees of the HBC and all related through blood or marriage, were early settlers in the Lac la Hache area of the Cariboo.

Archibald McKinlay, his wife Sarah Julia (nee Ogden), and their children took up a pre-emption on the east end of Lac la Hache in 1863. There they developed a cattle and horse ranch and kept a popular roadhouse for travellers on the wagon road. A fourth son, Duncan, was born at Lac la Hache in 1864, and when his parents retired to live in Savona with their married daughter Sarah in the early 1880s, he and his older brother Archie took over the ranch, while Archie's wife Mary (nee Ogden) operated the roadhouse.

James McKinlay, the eldest son, lost his young life to thieves who robbed and killed him on his return from selling a band of horses at the coast. Allen McKinlay, the third son, rode shotgun for the BC Express Company stagecoaches and was seldom at home.

The two McKinlay daughters, Sarah and Catherine, were both married—Sarah to Adam Ferguson of Savona and Catherine to Thomas McDougall. The McDougalls also lived at Lac la Hache for some time and had several children. When Catherine died giving birth to a fifth son, William, the child was adopted by her brother Archibald McKinlay and his wife Mary (left). William spent his life at the 115 Mile Ranch, where he died in 1959.

On Archie's death in 1919, Duncan McKinlay (right) assumed his brother's role while his sister-in-law Mary continued to operate the roadhouse until the ranch was sold to Bordy Felker in 1941. The 115 Mile House burned down in 1953.

Above are members of the second generation of the McKinlay family: Duncan (right) and his sister-in-law Mary (Ogden) McKinlay (left).

Archibald and Sarah Julia McKinlay started the 115 Mile Ranch and roadhouse in 1862. The family remained on the ranch for the next eight years. It was finally sold to George (Bordy) Felker in 1941. The roadhouse was destroyed by fire in 1953. Inset is the 1900 floor plan of the roadhouse.

The 122 Mile House

Constructed of enormous logs felled on site in 1867, the 122 Mile House was the last of several roadhouses built by the Walters brothers. Having passed through several hands, by 1893 the ranch and roadhouse were purchased by George Forbes, originally of Scotland, who, with his wife and six children, operated it until the mid-1930s.

The top photo, taken at the 122 Mile House in the spring of 1930, shows a caravan of cars on a journey from Seattle to Hazelton. The caravan was the inspiration of Premier Tolmie, and it was intended to bring together Canadian, American, and Alaskan officials to consider an extension of the highway to the Yukon and Alaska. Eight cars made the journey, including several from the 1910 era.

Middle right, a BC Express Company stagecoach stops outside the 122 Mile House in the 1880s.

Below, the Forbes family, the last to operate the roadhouse. Left to right: (back row) Gilbert, Muriel, Ethel, Gordon; (front row) Myrtle, Mrs. Forbes, Walter, George Forbes.

The 127 Mile House

Established in 1863 by Henry Felker, in 1867, when this Dally photo (bottom left) was taken, the "Blue Tent" Ranch and roadhouse was the property of William Wright. William's son John, who lived at the 137 Mile House, acquired the ranch in 1880 when he and his young wife Alice (shown top left) exchanged properties with Michael McCarthy.

Over the years twelve children were born to the Wrights, all of whom helped in the operation of the roadhouse and ranch. Both the original roadhouse and a second house (built during the First World War) burned down. The present house, built in 1916, is an example of an early pre-fab house bought from the T. Eaton Company.

Following the death of her mother, the youngest daughter, Gertrude, inherited the ranch and later married William Dingwall. The Wright family remained on the ranch until 1983, when it was sold to Wendall Monical of the 105 Mile Ranch.

Lawrence Boitanio (right) of Springhouse sits on "Brownie" outside the original roadhouse at the 127 Mile House. Built by Henry Felker in 1863, this house burned down in 1904. Lawrence, brother of legendary Williams Lake stampeder Antone, died young in 1914, the same year as his pioneer father Augustine, the long-time keeper of Springhouse on the original packer's trail.

John Wright (left) was twelve when he first came to the 127 Mile House from Ontario with his father William, his stepmother Katherine (Pratt), and her grown son David.

Lower right, the present-day house on the 127 Mile Ranch.

The 134 Mile House

Although, in general, roadhouses on the Cariboo Wagon Road were spaced at ten- or fifteen-mile intervals, in the Lac la Hache area between the 115 Mile House and the 150 Mile House there were at least a dozen or more between 1862 and the 1930s.

The 134 Mile House, built by Peter Eddy and his wife Elizabeth in 1862, was used as a roadhouse only until 1866, when, deep in debt, the Eddys' assets were sold at auction. Following this the house was used as a stage depot by the BC Express Company. The building burned down in 1960.

137 Mile House

The 137 Mile House (right), one of the few roadhouses still standing, was built by Michael McCarthy in the 1870s. Added on to in 1972 (middle), the house now contains many modern conveniences.

In this 1943 photo, a classic Cariboo Russell fence parallels the dirt road that connected northern British Columbia to the coast.

The 144 Mile House

William Phillip (above), the youngest boy of Antonette Felker's six children, was being treated for cancer when he met his future wife. Always fragile, Will Felker died in an upstairs bedroom of the 144 Mile House (below) in 1902. And ever after, until it was consumed by fire in 1964, the roadhouse was said to be haunted by Will's ghost. Fanny Leech (above right), who married Will Felker in 1899 and went to live at the roadhouse, was an extremely talented musician with very Bohemian ways. Unable to get along with her mother-in-law, Fanny, along with Will, moved out to a small house nearby, where two sons were born. Following Will Felker's death, Fanny became the wife of Alphonse Faucault, a freighter on the Cariboo Wagon Road, and lived for some years in the community of Walhachin.

The 150 Mile House

Having sold his roadhouse farm at Williams Lake in 1861, Thomas Davidson pre-empted land ten miles to the east, at what was to become the 150 milepost. There he built a large, two-storey log roadhouse beside the trail to the Cariboo, an enterprise that lasted for over 50 years. Davidson himself remained there for only a few years; then there began a long succession of owners, most of whom did well before selling the property off at a profit. To be successful, roadhouses had to be part of a self-sufficient farm that produced almost all their essential supplies and foods. At the 150 Mile House Ranch, which included over 1,000 acres of land, everything from beef cattle to dairy products and vegetables was produced. Seen here are two owners and an associate of the 150 Mile House.

Top and bottom, early photos of the 150 Mile House.

Top right, photo of Jerome Harper, cattleman, who, along with owner Edward Tormey, had an interest in the roadhouse during the 1860s. Middle, photo of Aschel S. Bates, who owned the roadhouse from 1871 to 1878, when he sold out to Gavin Hamilton (lower right), a retired HBC chief trader from Fort St. James.

During the early 1900s and prior to the rise of Williams Lake in 1919, 150 Mile was an important centre. In addition to the hotel and store were the headquarters of the police and magistrate, and a telegraph office. Along the highway and opposite the hotel, a number of small businesses sprang up.

These four photos (right) of the 150 Mile Hotel, store, and community were taken within the space of twelve years. The second photo, facing northwest with the bridge over Valley Creek in the foreground, was taken in 1898, while Vieth and Borland owned the complex. On the far right is a typical Russell fence

The third photo shows the 150 Mile House (or "White House," as it was also known) circa 1911, when it was operated by the Cariboo Trading Company of England.

The fourth photo, shows the 150 Mile store (with Bob Borland on the far right) and an early motoring party. Cars were just starting to make their appearance, and horses and freight wagons were still in use up until the late 1920s. Following the sale of the 150 Mile Ranch and hotel to the Cariboo Trading Company in 1900, extensive renovations were made to the buildings. The hotel burned to the ground in February of 1916.

Below are two of the Cariboo's characters: on the left, Chrissey Glassey, who married Bob Borland in his dotage and spent all his money; on the right, Fanny Leech, the eccentric wife of Will Felker.

Horsefly: First Known as Harper's Camp

The Little Horsefly River is known as the site of the Cariboo's first rich gold strike in 1859. During the 1890s another profitable but short-lived gold rush took place at nearby Harper's Camp, on the Horsefly River. Named for entrepreneur Thaddeus Harper, the town at this time supported two hotels, Alex Meiss's City Hotel and Harry Walters's Horsefly Hotel.

Henry L. Walters, whose family had a long history of roadhouse keeping on the Cariboo Road, settled at Horsefly in the 1890s, where he married eighteen-year-old Alva Youngker, a resident of 150 Mile. In 1897 Harry built the Horsefly Hotel, a three-storey log building with a bar room, dining room, parlour, and eight bedrooms. The Horsefly post office was housed in the hotel until 1905. Built during Horsefly's mining era, for several years the hotel provided meals for hungry mine workers. Harry and Alva Walters had eight children, all of whom helped out with various chores around the hotel, including the maintenance of a one-acre vegetable garden. Walters's Horsefly Hotel burned down in 1916. Following the death of Harry Walters in 1918, his widow married Alexander B. Campbell, also of Horsefly.

Pictured below is the Walters home at Horsefly. Inset photos show Harry L. Walters and his wife Alva Youngker.

The Walters home and hotel, circa 1912 (right). Built in two phases the houses accommodated both the large Walters family and their hotel guests.

Williams Lake

In many ways Williams Lake's emergence as the hub of the Cariboo in the 1920s has to do with location. After the First World War, with the pending arrival of the PGE and the junction of the Cariboo and Chilcotin Roads, Williams Lake's fate as the region's main trading centre was sealed. The addition of stockyards and a few lumber mills only confirmed its destiny.

In one sense, the Williams Lake of the mid-1920s was more new than old. While the Log Cabin Hotel, poised strategically near the new PGE Railway station, bore the markings of an earlier era, most other buildings looked new and prosperous. Change sounded with the arrival of the PGE steam engines. The upper roadhouse on the Pinchbeck Ranch, which was last occupied by Mamie Comer (left) and her brothers, was torn down in 1925 and its many parts were used in the buildings of the new community of Williams Lake. Following Pinchbeck's death in 1893, his ranch was seized by creditors and leased to Joseph P. Patenaude and his sons, Albert and Ernest. The Patenaude family worked both the upper and lower ranches for five years before it was sold to Robert Borland, co-owner of the 150 Mile Ranch. Borland lived in the lower house and leased the upper ranch to the Comers. By 1919 Borland had sold the ranch to the PGE. At this time the lower house became a roadhouse, where railway employees were boarded. By 1930 the lower house, like the upper house before it, had been torn down and its parts used in the building of several new houses around Williams Lake.

Williams Lake (top), Railway Avenue after 1921, with the railway station on the left, the Log Cabin Hotel on the right, and Moore's store in the middle.

Mamie Comer (middle left), Robert Borland (inset left), and Joseph Patenaude (inset right), who started the Masonic Lodge in Williams Lake.

Pinchbeck's lower house (below) at the foot of Williams Lake.

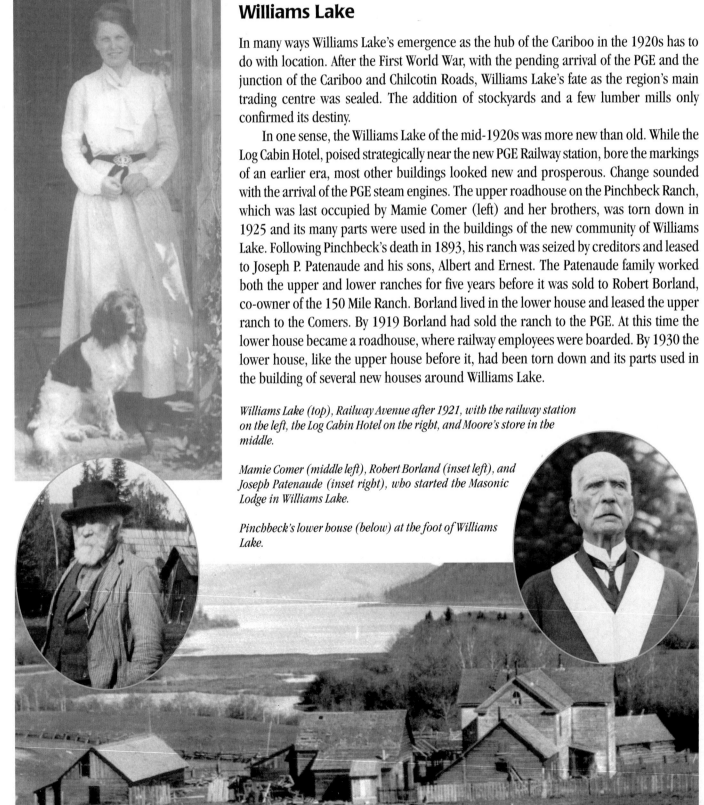

Mr. Rife, the local druggist, was also the photographer who, circa 1925, took many of the photos that appear on this page.

Top (from the left): Elliot's butcher shop, a temporary athletic hall, Fraser and McKenzie's store, and the Lakeview Hotel in the early 1920s (shortly before being destroyed by a major fire).

Above (left to right): the PGE station house and Rife's Drug Store.
Right: Williams Lake looking south on Railway Avenue. This was the original road into Williams Lake prior to the building of a bypass, in the late 1950s, on the south end of the town.

Bottom (from the left): Railway Avenue, Log Cabin Hotel, McKenzie's store, and the Lakeview Hotel (far right).

Williams Lake North: The Merging of Three Trails to Gold

It was the search for fur, and then gold, that enticed people to travel deep into the interior of British Columbia. At first travel was by water, then by several different overland routes. The fur traders of the early 1800s and the first miners of 1859 travelled by way of the Fraser River, upstream from Lillooet as far as Fort Alexandria and the mouth of the Quesnel River. By land the packers followed the Native trail north from Lillooet, or Parsonsville, upriver to Williams Lake, which had been used by HBC fur traders on their way to Fort St. James. From Williams Lake, some travellers continued north along the river trail to Fort Alexandria, while others veered east to what is now 150 Mile House and north to Deep Creek, Beaver Lake, and the Quesnel River. By the fall of 1859 all trails had converged on the Quesnel River and Quesnel Forks, the first permanent gold camp.

Those who travelled north on the river trail from Williams Lake would have found refuge at a stopping house just south of Soda Creek known as Springfield Ranch, pre-empted by John F. Hawkes and his partner John Calbraith (who had been a partner of G.B. Wright, the road contractor). The famous Judge Matthew Baillie Begbie, who travelled this route on his assize circuits, often stayed there.

The original 1863 wagon road was built due north of the 150 Mile House up an eight-mile grade. The steep grade would prove a two-day undertaking for most freighters and their heavily laden wagons. While a ranch and roadhouse known as Carpenter's House had operated along this route in the 1860s, it did not last long (although there is still a Carpenters Mountain). Another early but short-lived roadhouse was Frank Way's 164 Mile House at Deep Creek.

153 Mile Ranch, Roadhouse, and Store

Three miles from the 150 Mile Ranch another roadhouse farm began to develop in the early 1900s. Situated on an accommodating flat halfway up the mountain, this roadhouse, along with a popular store, was established in 1902 by Louis and Clara Crosina. After many years of operation the ranch passed from the Crosinas' daughter, Lily, to Joseph Ernest Patenaude in the 1950s. The store is now a private museum, open by appointment.

Willie Crosina stands at the entrance to the family ranch in this picture taken prior to 1914. The original store (built in 1902) is seen in the right background.

Matthew Baillie Begbie (above) was appointed the first judge of British Columbia on September 4, 1858. His name became synonymous with goldfield justice until 1879, when he retired from the assize circuit.

The house at Springfield Ranch. Calbraith and Hawke's farm, circa 1865. Note the sod roof on the log building.

The 158 Mile House

It was not until the late 1880s, when Steven Tingley was in need of land on which to pasture some of his stagecoach horses, that another roadhouse complex came into being at the 158 milepost. Situated at the junction of the roads to Horsefly, Likely, and Soda Creek, for a time the roadhouse enjoyed a large clientele. More commonly known as the Mountain House, the ranch was for a time leased by Louis Crosina and his bride, Clara Noble, a local schoolteacher. Other owners of this landmark location were William Parker of Big Lake and Louis Crosina and his son Willie. The roadhouse burned down in 1943.

Seen above is the roadhouse, and seated on the porch in this 1921 photo are (left to right) Tommy Comer, Ernie Long, Ethel Hamilton, Dolly Crosina, Ivy Lock, Jack Davidson, Olive Lock, Bob Burgess, Louis Crosina (owner of the property at that time), Bill Lock, and Jimmy Hargreaves.

The 164 Mile House at Deep Creek

A few miles further along the road to Soda Creek, at the 164 milepost, Frank Way, with his partner G.B. Wright , developed a farm and built a roadhouse close to Deep Creek. Established in 1863, just as Wright's wagon road reached this point, Deep Creek House was, for a short time, an extremely busy place. However, after only two years a worsening economy forced Frank Way to flee the country. Owned by the Bank of British Columbia for some years, the farm and roadhouse were eventually purchased by Aschel Sumner Bates of 150 Mile House. By the 1870s this land had become part of the Deep Creek Indian Reserve.

The picture below was taken by Frederick Dally in 1867, while the roadhouse was operated by Aschel Bates.

Billy Lyne's 170 Mile House

Situated nine miles south of Soda Creek and beside the Cariboo Wagon Road, the site of the Lyne Ranch had long been a campground for freighters. Searching for a means of independence, William Lyne Jr. and his younger brother John (formerly of Williams Lake) moved to the site in 1889, where they made a living as blacksmiths catering to the freighters. Billy's wife Angelique, a strong-willed and capable young woman, began providing meals to the freighters from her little cabin on the new pre-emption, but it was 1896 before there was time for Billy and John to build a proper roadhouse. Of salt-box construction, the two-storey frame house was finally completed in 1912.

Along with her own five children, Angelique also raised several grandchildren while attending to the endless work of operating a roadhouse and ranch. Although the roadhouse business had subsided by the 1920s, the house itself remained until the 1970s, when new owners destroyed it to build a modern structure on the same site.

Seen right is a formal photograph of the Billy Lyne Jr. family, taken on the porch of the roadhouse in 1910. Behind Angelique and Billy are (from the left) Vivian, Edith, David, Ella, and Evelyn.

Below is a photo of Angelique (Dussault) Lyne taken in 1895. She is shown with four of her eventual five children.

Bottom left is the Lyne Ranch with the salt-box roadhouse (inset), the large barn, and, in the foreground, Lyne's sawmill.

Soda Creek

Prior to the building of Wright's wagon road to Soda Creek, pack trains travelled to the goldfields by way of what became the 150 Mile House and then headed north to Beaver Lake and the Quesnel River. At first it was thought that this would be the path of the wagon road, but it contained too many swamps and had too much low ground to be practical. Once the road was built to Alexandria, traffic went by way of Soda Creek and then north either by the sternwheel steamer *Enterprise* or by the rough trail past Fort Alexandria to Quesnellemouth (which is what Quesnel was first called in order to avoid its being confused with Quesnel Forks).

Just two miles north of Soda Creek, the Dunlevy Ranch and roadhouse, through which ran the HBC brigade trail, had been established before the wagon road was built. The area from Soda Creek north to Macalister, a distance of fifteen miles, contained some of the most arable and ideally situated farm land in the Cariboo. It was, of course, pre-empted very early in the 1860s. Along here was the Pickard Ranch, also an early pre-emption, which was developed in the early 1900s by George Pickard, a part Welsh and part French voyageur who had followed his uncle west from New Brunswick.

Robert McLeese's Colonial Hotel (above) at Soda Creek.

To the right is a photo of downtown Soda Creek in the 1870s, showing both the Colonial Hotel and Dunlevy's Exchange Hotel. Note how close they are to one another.

Below is a close-up of Dunlevy's Exchange Hotel, built by George Hendricks in 1863 and purchased by Dunlevy and his associates that same year.

Tragedy at Soda Creek

When news of the building of a sternwheel steamship on the upper Fraser reached New Westminster in 1861 it caused great excitement among the business population of the Lower Mainland, who looked upon it as a great opportunity for the future. Wasting no time, Robert McLeese and his partner Joseph T. Senay set out for Soda Creek, where they secured a building lot close to the steamboat landing and proceeded to build a two-and-one-half storey log structure known as the Colonial Hotel. Directly beside them was a second hotel, the Exchange, which had been built for Peter Dunlevy. By 1863, with the steamer SS *Enterprise* in operation, the little community of Soda Creek became a hive of industry and enterprise. The Colonial Hotel was still doing a thriving business in 1868 when Joseph Senay was married in Victoria to Annie Wall and, following a short honeymoon, returned with his bride to Soda Creek. Barely a year later, while crossing the Quesnel River at Quesnel, a tragic accident occurred, the ferry capsized, and Annie Senay was drowned. Joseph Senay was so heartbroken that he gave up his partnership in the hotel, resigned as postmaster, and left Soda Creek for the Lower Mainland.

Pictured here are Joseph Triffle Senay (left) and Robert McLeese (right), partners in the Colonial Hotel at Soda Creek.

Below (left) are the two hotels at Soda Creek, with the SS Enterprise *in the foreground (c. 1868).*

North to Peter Dunlevy's Ranch And Roadhouse, 1862

Following their rich strike of gold on Little Horsefly Creek in 1859, Peter Dunlevy and his four partners invested their wealth in roadhouses and freighting outfits. When news broke of the building of a sternwheel ship on the upper Fraser River in 1862, Dunlevy took up 640 acres of land just north of Soda Creek, which became the southern terminus of the steamship. There he developed many acres of grain and built a large log roadhouse, which was in operation beside the Cariboo trail even before the wagon road was built. The house, in a dilapidated state, stood until 1987, when the present owners of the property demolished it.

Pickards And Their Children

Arriving at Mackin Creek in 1890, the Pickards and their seven children lived in a small log cabin until a larger, two-storey house was built in 1900. The 160-acre Pickard Ranch lay north of the original Dunlevy Ranch, near the junction of the old pack trail and wagon road. It welcomed many travellers during the first half of the century.

Above is a Dally photo of the Dunlevy Ranch at harvest time. Notice the heavy crop of grain. Below is Pickard's House, or the 173 Mile House, seven miles north of Soda Creek. Inset is a portion of the Dunlevy roadhouse just prior to its demolition.

East of Soda Creek: Beaver Lake, Big Lake, and Mud Lake

Through the years, three significant roadhouses and ranches were welcome destinations for the weary traveller. The oldest, which dates back to the pack routes, was Beaver Lake House. Built in 1860 on the first Cariboo lands ever pre-empted, this site was the junction of many trails that merged here before continuing northeast into the mountains. Peter Dunlevy and his partner James Sellers acquired the original and only log structure there and established a successful roadhouse and trading post.

Beaver Lake went through periods of prosperity and decline over the ensuing years, but enjoyed a strong resurgence in the 1890s, when mining activity in the region was strong. A "new house" was built by Frank Guy in 1896, and this building remained a popular roadhouse/hunting lodge well into the 1950s.

Beaver Lake and Beaver Lake House

The Beaver Lake site in a tranquil, rural valley 30 miles east of McLeese Lake offered the last opportunity for miners and packers to obtain feed and supplies before heading up into the mountains towards the Quesnel River. Here two 1860 pre-emptions by three Frenchmen were the first registered land claims in the Cariboo. The Frenchmen operated a roadhouse, store, and saloon where liquor was sold and bags of gold changed hands frequently over the gambling tables. By 1870 the much-enlarged Beaver Lake Ranch was owned by French Canadian packer Frank Guy and his Chinese partner Ah Tom. Prior to Frank Guy's death in 1898, the ranch was sold to Clifford W. Eagle of Williams Lake. When Eagle went to war in 1915, he put his sister Christine Hamilton and her husband Gavin Hamilton in charge of the ranch. There they lived for many years in the large roadhouse. The building burned down in February of 1971.

Beaver Lake roadhouse (below), built in 1896. Frank Guy (inset left) successfully operated the Beaver Lake Ranch for 28 years. Christine Eagle Hamilton and her husband Gavin Hamilton (inset right) at Beaver Lake in 1950.

Bill Parker's Big Lake Ranch and Roadhouse

While land at Big Lake was first pre-empted in 1862, it was soon abandoned when the wagon road to the goldfields was built by way of Soda Creek and Quesnel. In 1896, with the resurgence of mining in the Quesnel Dam and Horsefly area of the Cariboo, a quiet young man from Wisconsin, William Parker, started a ranch at Big Lake, halfway between the 150 Mile House and Quesnel Forks. There he built a popular roadhouse that was operated by his housekeeper, Mrs. McNutt, who also ran the post office.

In earlier years Parker had been a stage driver for the BX Company and sometimes rode shotgun while transporting gold bullion to the bank in Ashcroft. By 1900 Parker had incorporated his own stage line and, armed with the mail contract, transported passengers and freight between Ashcroft, Keithley Creek, and Quesnel Forks. On one trip the brakes of his wagon train failed, and he lost everything over the edge of Clinton hill. It was said that sabotage was involved, and it ended Parker's stage line. Bill never married, and as he grew older he lost his hearing and took to communicating by means of written notes. He died in his sleep at his home in Big Lake in 1927 at the age of 67. The old Parker roadhouse was taken down in 1985, and now only the blacksmith shop and saddle shed remain.

A formal photograph of William Parker as a young man.

Mud Lake

In one of his voluminous letters to Governor Douglas, Gold Commissioner Philip H. Nind wrote of a journey that he and his constable, William Pinchbeck, had made to Quesnel Forks in September of 1860. By way of the HBC brigade trail from Williams Lake they travelled 20 miles north to Mud Lake, where they came across the store and cattle pasture of Joel Palmer, the original settler in this location. A year later Joel had new neighbours.

Winter comes early to the Cariboo, especially in the mountains. Having made themselves rich over the short season of 1861, many miners departed for warmer climates. In November of that year, as they made their way south, James May and George Weaver speculated on land southeast of Mud Lake. They each pre-empted 160 acres and had houses built. Their investments paid off the following year when their properties were purchased. Entrepreneurs Peter Dunlevy and James Sellers built a large log roadhouse beside the brigade trail. The roadhouse farm at Mud Lake was a very busy place until 1865, when the gold rush ebbed.

In 1985 some of the logs from Mud Lake House were discovered piled up in a farmer's field. Said to have been logged from the site, they were enormous, clear, squared timbers measuring approximately 22 inches by 10 inches by 40 feet in length.

James May, among the first discoverers of Cariboo gold in 1859.

Below, the Big Lake stopping house and post office, circa 1895.

The Original Route to the Goldfields:
Beaver Lake to Snowshoe Mountain

Little Lake Ranch and Prior's Roadhouse

The origins of the Little Lake Ranch, sixteen miles northeast of Beaver Lake, date back to an 1860 roadhouse near a trail to the Quesnel River ferry. During the 1890s, this abandoned site was pre-empted again, by entrepreneurs George Vieth and Robert Borland, who used it as a slaughterhouse for beef sold to the nearby Bullion Mine.

In 1910 Samuel Crabtree Prior, a young English butcher who had worked for a decade at Little Lake, married Emily Eholt, the daughter of the foreman at the Bullion Mine. The Priors re-established a stopping house on the ranch and catered to travellers on their way to and from Quesnel Dam, now known as Likely. Over the years two Prior children, Joseph and Bernice, were born and

grew up at Little Lake. A post office known as "Hydraulic" opened in 1913, with Sam Prior as postmaster — a position he held for 47 years. Following his death in 1960, a certificate of appreciation was posthumously awarded to Sam for his long years of postal service. Although the roadhouse business had long since ceased, Emily Prior continued to live on the farm until her death in 1981, when she was over 90 years of age.

Seen below, in a 1975 photo taken by the author, is the Little Lake Ranch and roadhouse. Inset (c. 1947) shows, right to left, Sam Prior, his wife Emily, and his daughter Bernice. On the left is Joe Poirier, Bernice's first husband, who died in 1969.

Quesnel Forks

Known as the first permanent settlement of the Cariboo gold rush of 1859 Quesnel Forks, at the confluence of the north and south forks of the Quesnel River, became the gateway to the discovery of many famous gold creeks in that vicinity. By 1861 a town consisting of log buildings, and a bridge had been built across the south fork of the river by Samuel Adler and Thomas Barry, who also operated Bridge House, a very popular place of entertainment. Following the exodus of Europeans in the 1870s, a community of Chinese miners occupied Quesnel Forks, where they lived and practised their own religion and culture for the next 40 years. With a resurgence of mining on the Quesnel River during the 1890s several Europeans returned to the "Forks," where they once again opened stores and hotels. Today, although most of the buildings have fallen down, some restoration work is being done through a government grant. The town has yet to be declared a heritage site.

In 1949 three tourists pose with Lim Sing in front of Quesnel Forks's only remaining store, which was built by Sing's father in 1881.

Sam Adler (inset), with his partner Thomas Barry, built a tollbridge across the river at Quesnel Forks in the 1860s and operated a saloon known as Bridge House. Below is a photo of Quesnel Forks in the 1880s in which the bridge (inset left) is hidden by the hillside in the left foreground.

Keithley Creek

Operated by George Vieth and Robert Borland for nearly 50 years between 1870 and the early 1900s, the Keithley Creek Ranch has become an historical landmark. The pencil sketch on the right (executed by the author) depicts the ranch buildings of the 1980s. The original roadhouse burned down in 1889, taking with it all the old records and artifacts. A second roadhouse (seen below) burned down in 1935.

Among those seen in the photo below are Mrs. Laylander, Harry Heur, Dave Lowden, Tom and Anne Williams, Mabel Borland, Betty Gorrie, Wiff Ray, Mike Gillis, Anna and George Eop, Ernie Lang, Mr. Andresien, and George Harrison. Bob Borland, who died in 1923, is buried in the Keithley Creek Cemetery close to the ranch.

Snowshoe Mountain and Yanks Peak

During the early years of the Cariboo gold rush a prospector and miner named William Luce, of Maine, staked claims and lived close to his workings on a branch of Snowshoe Mountain northeast of Keithley Creek.

His cabin, which was beside the pack-train trail, became a roadhouse visited not only by miners, but also, during the 1870s, by a reporter from the Barkerville *Cariboo Sentinel*. The reporter found William Luce to be an interesting subject and over a period of several years wrote a number of reports about him. It was due to these reports of his exploits that Luce was first given the title "the Live Yank." Upon his death in May of 1881, Luce's family in the United States paid for a wooden headboard that was to be placed on his grave, close to his cabin. The board was carved by Johnny Knott of Barkerville and, when completed, was given to Fred Littler, the postal worker in the area, for delivery. The headboard was cumbersome and difficult to keep lashed to a pack mule, so, after adjusting it several times, Littler, in a fit of exasperation, threw it down in the vicinity of Sawmill Flat on Antler Creek. There it remained until 1939, when it was discovered, restored, and transported to its intended resting-place on Luce Creek.

But this was not the end of the story. Over the years the site of Luce's grave was obliterated by modern mining, and the headboard was lost once more. During the 1950s it was retrieved by a sheepherder, who found it wired to a tree on the flanks of Yanks Peak (named for William Luce). While the lettering was still discernible, weathering had split the board lengthwise. This original artifact is now on display in the Williams Lake Museum.

Seen here is a drawing (by the author) of the original 1881 headboard and an 1863 photo of William Luce.

The Reverend R.J. Dundas at Maloney's Roadhouse: A Brush with a Criminal

On a small alpine meadow near the headwaters of Antler Creek, miner Thomas Maloney built a cabin beside the trail leading to Williams Creek. By October of 1861 Maloney had pre-empted 80 acres of land at this site, where his cabin had become a popular roadhouse. The outlines of Maloney's roadhouse, which operated between 1861 and 1866, are still visible. It was a large building, but all that remains of it today is a pile of rubble that was once its stone fireplace. With the completion of the wagon road from Quesnellemouth to Barkerville in 1865, traffic along the Antler trail declined and Tom Maloney moved on.

During the Cariboo gold rush, in 1862, the Anglican Church bishop George Hills and his clerics, the Reverend Robert J. Dundas (right) and the Reverend C. Knipe, travelled from Victoria to the goldfields to minister to the miners. Both Bishop Hills and Reverend Dundas kept detailed diaries of their experiences, and it is from this source that the following information is derived. While Knipe remained at Van Winkle and Bishop Hills at Williams Creek, Dundas was stationed in the town of Antler Creek.

One morning, while on his way to see the bishop at Williams Creek, Dundas stopped in at Maloney's for breakfast. Unaware that he was doing so, he sat down at the same table as did a known criminal, Liverpool Jack, who at that very moment was being pursued by the local police for a crime he had committed the night before. While they were eating, someone at the door alerted the criminal to an approaching constable, and Liverpool Jack rose up suddenly, flew out the rear of the house, and disappeared into the nearby woods. Dundas, who was very new to the country, was visibly shaken when he realized what was going on.

Reverend Dundas also visited Maloney's a second time to assist Bishop Hills with a funeral. John Emmory, a miner at Williams Creek who died in August of 1862, had asked to be buried next to a dear friend who had died and been buried near Maloney's the year before. The two graves, situated on a rise of ground just north of Maloney's, may still be seen today. The name of Emmory's friend is not known.

Above is the Rhubarb Cabin at the headwaters of Antler Creek. Perched on top of many feet of hand-piled tailings, for Antler Creek was very rich in gold, the cabin is named for a rhubarb patch and several chive plants that grow perennially a few feet away. This typical miner's cabin has been abandoned for some years.

This 1865 E.M. Richardson sketch (left) was made on Grouse Creek as the artist pursued the gold rush.

The Wagon Road North: Alexandria to Quesnel

G.B. Wright's contract to build a wagon road from Clinton to Alexandria was completed in August of 1863. Exactly where the road ended is uncertain, but it was close to the site of Fort Alexandria, where now stands the Alexandria Indian Reserve. When the government put out tenders for the building of the remaining 30-odd miles of road to Quesnel that year, no one applied, least of all G.B. Wright, who had launched the first sternwheel steamboat in the upper Fraser. This accommodating little boat took all the passengers and freight it could and, in its first year of operation, more than recovered its construction cost. Finally, during the summer of 1865, Robert T. (Peg-Leg) Smith contracted to build the road, which was completed in September. Between Alexandria and Quesnel there were seven roadhouse farms, the first of which was McInnes House.

McInnes House

Originally a part of the North West Company's fur depot at Alexandria in 1814, this building was enlarged in 1873 and turned into a stopping house on the Cariboo Wagon Road by Alexander Douglas McInnes. Attracted by the Cariboo gold rush, McInnes first came to Williams Creek in 1863, where he had a share in the famous Cameron claim. Following his marriage to Elizabeth Roddy, he and his wife kept a boarding house for the men working in the mine. From there the McInneses moved to Van Winkle on Lightning Creek, where they kept another boarding house.

By the 1870s, and with four children in tow, the McInneses took up what had been HBC land near Fort Alexandria, about 40 miles south of Quesnel. Their roadhouse was very successful and was in operation for many years. Following the death of her parents, the McInneses' married daughter, Mary Rowed, inherited the property, where she kept the roadhouse and post office until her death in 1937. When McInnes House fell into ruin during the 1940s, plans were made to restore it. Unfortunately, although intentions were good, the work was never done.

Seen here are (left) Mary McInnes Rowed in front of McInnes House (c. 1900), (right) her father Alexander Douglas McInnes, and (bottom) the remains of McInnes House in the 1940s.

Anders's Roadhouse: The 188 Mile House

Upon the death of her brother William Pinchbeck in 1893, Annie Anders and her husband William left Williams Lake to establish a roadhouse farm at the 188 Mile on the Cariboo Wagon Road. The two-storey frame house of salt-box design catered to passengers aboard the BC Express Company stagecoach and to the local Natives, who came to trade at Anders's store. The Natives had a particular fondness for Mrs. Anders's hard-boiled candies, which, in 1903, she made in her own kitchen. The Anders invited their nephew William Broughton to come out from England to assist Mr. Anders on the farm. A year later, William's fiancee Ada Littlewood arrived, and they were married. Tragically, a year after William Broughton Jr. was born, his father died. In 1913 Ada married Frank Aiken, a provincial policeman. Following the death of Mr. and Mrs. Anders, the Aikens inherited the farm, where they brought up several children. Edward Aiken, who had remained on the property, and his wife Marie Vasseur were the last of the original family to operate the roadhouse. The house has been declared beyond restoration.

Pictured top right is William J. Anders with Ada Littlewood in the background. This couple kept a roadhouse beside the Cariboo Wagon road for many years at the 188 milepost.

Pictured middle right is Ada (Littlewood) Broughton and her son Willie Broughton Jr., Annie Pinchbeck Anders and her husband William.

Seen below is the Broughton Ranch north of the Anders property. The third ranch home (inset) was built in 1906 by Bob Yorston. The ranch borders the Fraser River.

The Australian Ranch

There have been three roadhouses on the Australian Ranch. The first was abandoned shortly after it was built in 1863; the second burned down in 1906; and the third was badly damaged in most unusual circumstances in the spring of 1955.

Originally the Cariboo Wagon Road had passed through the ranch, but by the 1950s a new road had been built to the east on higher ground well above the flat where all the buildings were situated. Heavy winter snows and a warm spring caused high water levels in 1955. When the culvert designed to carry the water off the highway failed, a lake built up behind it, eventually undermining the road. It spilled on to the flat land, covering the buildings with twelve feet of water. As the wall of water hit the old roadhouse, it splashed against the second-storey windows but, strangely enough, did not break them. Mud, rocks, and water battered the 50-year-old structure, knocking it off its moorings. Only the weight of the two brick chimneys steadied it, bringing it to rest in a tangle of telephone wires.

Once the water subsided the bed of Australian Creek had to be rerouted and most of the buildings on the ranch had to be repaired. The roadhouse continued to be occupied by part of the Yorston family and, later, by labourers.

Above, an annual Australian Ranch picnic tradition (which is still upheld) was first inaugurated to celebrate the arrival from England of most of the local residents on July 1, 1904. In the landmark picture shown above are (in the back, from the left) Mr. Anders, Mrs George Broughton, Tommy Roddie, Henry Windt Sr., Ella Windt (who was by this time Mrs. Roddy Moffat), Johnny Webster, Frank Broughton, Mrs. Janet Yorston, Billy Webster, Henry Windt Jr., Emily Webster, Jack Yorston Sr., Tommy Windt, George Windt, Fritz Menzinger, and Henry Moffat Jr.; (front row, left to right) Lily Windt, Mrs. Ethel Yorston with baby daughter, Mrs. Windt Sr., Mrs. Ada (Broughton) Aiken, Mrs. Anders with little Willie Broughton, and Mrs. Gladstone (Mrs. Windt's mother).

Quesnel: Front Street

When G.B. Wright's sternwheeler from Soda Creek first landed at Quesnel in 1863 it marked the beginning of a resourceful future for the new community. Two years later, after the wagon road had reached town, Quesnel quickly established itself as the main Fraser River trading centre north of Lillooet, and Front Street became a hive of commerce.

In 1865 (top), looking up from the steamboat landing, buildings include James Reed's warehouse, Goudie's BC Express Company office, the Bank of BC, G.B. Wright's (later the Hudson's Bay Company store) and Reid's General Store, a drugstore, and (with flagpoles and upper verandah) the original Occidental Hotel.

In 1910 (middle), looking down Front Street to the Fraser River, the New Cariboo Hotel in the foreground and the second Occidental Hotel helped confirm Quesnel as the centre of Cariboo commerce.

This 1890 photo was taken on Front Street during a celebration. Behind the trees is the first Occidental Hotel, and to the left, the location of the first (but temporary) school in the early 1880s.

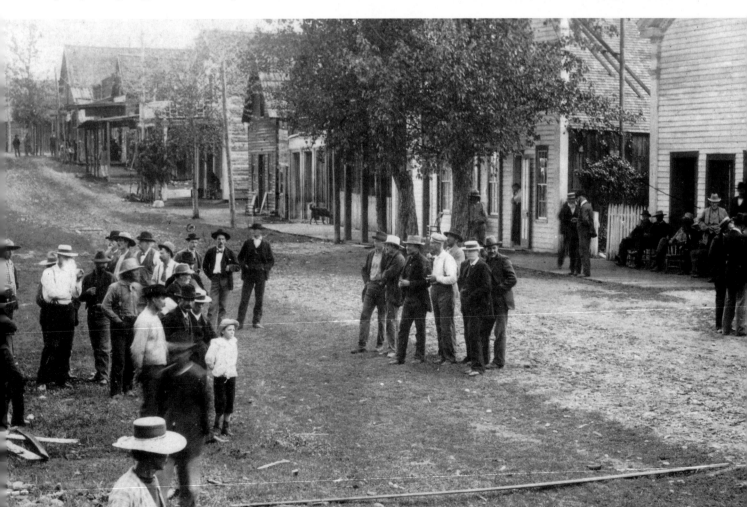

For almost six decades, sternwheelers brought cargo and adventurers from the south. Here (c. 1915), the SS Quesnel, SS BC Express, and SS BX share the base of Front Street.

Of the twenty children in Ethel Robertson's 1903 classroom, six were Moffats; four each were Carsons and Wintrips, respectively; and two were Johnstons.

A 1911 postcard documented Quesnel's first street light, located on Carson Avenue. The Carson blacksmith shop and home are in the distance. A second pole site is planted near "Pop" Elliot's billiard hall.

The Occidental Hotels of Quesnel

The community of Quesnellemouth began in 1863, following the survey of a townsite by Royal Engineer William McColl. By 1865 several stores and a hotel were to be seen along the waterfront close to G.B. Wright's steamboat landing. Built by entrepreneurs Thomas Brown and Hugh Gillis, the Occidental Hotel soon became known as the best hotel on the Cariboo Wagon Road.

Following Thomas Brown's death, his widow Sarah married John McLean, a rich old miner. They leased out the hotel until 1907, when it was sold to businessman Edward Kepner of Seattle, Washington. Kepner soon tore down the original Occidental Hotel and built a lavish new four-storey hotel in its place. Included in the facility were a large dining room, a ballroom, a pool hall, and a saloon that never closed. Upstairs were accommodations for 50 people, and while the hotel did not have indoor plumbing, there was a two-storey outhouse at its back end. In January of 1916, when a fire destroyed almost all of the buildings along Front Street, the only thing left of the Occidental Hotel was the two-level outhouse. Despite the covering of embossed fireproof siding on its exterior, the building caught fire.

The original Occidental Hotel, with lanky John McLean standing on the upper level, is shown shortly before it was razed. John McLean (inset), a pioneer of Quesnel, was one of the original five white men who ascended the Fraser River in 1859 and managed to escape a Native massacre. He died in October 1915.

Below right is Front Street, prior to the First World War, with its two grand hotels and a row of meticulous storefronts.

The only thing to remain of the Occidental Hotel (left) after the devastating fire of January 1916 was the two-storey outhouse, seen behind the man on the right.

A 1915 photograph of the Occidental Hotel bar room and saloon (below left), shortly before the hotel burned down. Owner Edward Kepner is seen at the bar in his shirtsleeves. The band-riveted drum heater was typical of that era and consisted of one circulating drum above another.

Freighters transferring cargo from the riverboats at Quesnel and local farmers like H.H. Sing (above) were a common sight on the road between Quesnel and Barkerville well into the 1900s. Tandem wagons pulled by horses or mules were the choice of many.

The Road to Barkerville

The 10 Mile House

The flat of land ten miles east of Quesnel had at one time been an HBC campground, and in the 1860s it was the site of a Royal Engineers' campground prior to the building of the Cariboo Road. During the 1880s, while it was being used by freighters on their way to Barkerville, this land became the site of a roadhouse farm. Charles Laronde, a husky, good-looking Metis from Manitoba, and his Native wife, Marie Boucher, began cooking meals for the freighters, and before long Charlie built a sturdy squared log cabin that provided overnight accommodation. Marie's cooking added much to the reputation of the stopping place; especially enjoyed were her delicious blueberry pies topped with whipped cream.

As the roadhouse business increased during the 1890s, Charlie built three additions and a lean-to kitchen on to his original cabin. During the winter, when business was quiet, this hard-working couple ran a registered trapline, one of the first and largest in

the country. A talented fellow, Charlie also played the fiddle at local dances, tapping out the time with his left foot. As the years rolled by, Charlie was besieged with rheumatism and more or less became confined to home. With Charlie unable to work the trapline, Marie took over, bringing in the catches of beaver, mink, and marten. At home, Charlie attempted to cater to the freighters, but his cooking left a lot to be desired, and before long the clientele had dwindled to only the odd one. Prior to his death in 1919 Charlie became quite deranged, and he spent the last few years of his life in a mental institution in New Westminster.

Left are Charles Laronde and his wife Marie, with the 10 Mile House and its several additions in the background. So well built were these squared log and dovetailed buildings that when they were destroyed in 1960, most of the logs were still sound.

The 13 Mile House

First operated by Overlander Richard S. Cormack in 1864, the roadhouse depicted here was built by John Strand for Alexander Locke in 1900. This roadhouse was on the original wagon road, which is now bypassed, but the site is still visible from the present highway.

Originally from Ontario, "Sandy" Locke arrived in the Cariboo during the 1870s and took a job driving the BC Express Company stagecoaches between Quesnel and Barkerville.

The Lockes' establishment at the 13 milepost was a popular stagecoach stop during the early 1900s and soon gained a reputation for fine meals and for the kind attention of its owners. Mrs. Jean Locke, part of the well-known Kelly family of Barkerville, had been brought up with a keen knowledge of the roadhouse business. As a small child she had lived and worked at her parents' hotel. Jean and her sisters had also been fortunate enough to receive piano and singing lessons while they were growing up. At the 13 Mile House Jean and her children entertained their guests in the evenings with singing and piano recitals in the parlour of the roadhouse. Several of the eventual seven Locke children were born at the 13 Mile House, but by 1912, due to the need to find adequate schooling, the Locke family sold out and moved to Quesnel.

The second 13 Mile road-house, built in 1900 (top).

This watercolour sketch of the 13 Mile House (c. 1910) was painted from a photo-graph supplied to the author by Mrs. Laura Livingstone, the eldest of the Locke children.

A visit to the in-laws? Here, in 1911, the Locke family (bottom) set out for a sleigh ride on the main street of Barkerville.

Cottonwood House

The land on which Cottonwood House Provincial Park stands today was first pre-empted in 1863 by John Ryder, a freight driver. Ryder sold out soon after to his partner Allen Smith, a contractor involved in the building of the road to the goldfields. By 1864 Smith had started to build the roadhouse known today as Cottonwood House. For its first ten years the Cottonwood Ranch changed hands many times until finally, in 1874, it was purchased by John Boyd for $5,000.

John Boyd lived at Cottonwood House from 1886 until his death in March of 1909, while his wife Janet, who was much younger than he, lived on until January of 1940. The adjustment for the Boyd family following John's death was considerable, as hardly anything had ever been planned without his involvement.

From the 1860s on, John Boyd kept dozens of account books, journals, and daybooks, registering every transaction at both Cold Spring, Cottonwood House, and the store (including the wages of everyone who ever worked for him — even his own family members). And yet when John Boyd died, no will was ever found. Left with hardly anything in the estate's account, Mrs. Boyd immediately reduced all expenditures, including cooks and servants. Of the boys, only Willie and Harry were at home to carry on with the work. When Alice, the only remaining girl, was married to Jim Coreau in 1935, she and Jim continued to live at Cottonwood House until 1950. By this time, with both his mother and Willie gone, Harry sold out to Vagn Olrik. In 1961 the property was purchased by the provincial government, which declared it a heritage site in 1963.

Left is John Ryder, the original pre-emptor of the Cottonwood Ranch, and his family at Cheam, BC.

Right is Josiah C. Beedy, miner and entrepreneur, and his wife. Beedy and his partner Jochum W. Lindhard operated Cottonwood House during the early 1870s.

Below is Cottonwood House (the car is a "stage," or taxi, that travelled between Quesnel and Barkerville). On the left behind the car is Willie Boyd, who died in 1939, and in front is John Lazzarin Jr., a long-time resident of Quesnel.

The Town That Was Wingdam

Wingdam, an area a few miles east of Cottonwood, first gained attention in the 1870s when John Boyd and several of his associates staked hard-rock gold claims north and west along Lightning Creek. They formed the Big Bonanza Mining Company and, with limited success, worked the claims for many years. Wingdam was named for the wooden "wings" used to divert the waters of Lightning Creek. Mining was difficult here, due to seepage and unpredictable water supply. Anticipating continued development, John Fleming, a brother to Mrs. John Boyd, pre-empted a nearby 160-acre flat of land in August of 1899. By then various buildings were already on the flat, several of them roadhouses used by freighters on their way to Barkerville.

During the depression of the 1930s Wingdam grew almost large enough to become a town. Prospectors and transients lived in temporary log and frame buildings and mined for gold in Lightning Creek. Some were employed in the Wingdam Mine, which was operated by Consolidated Gold Alluvials of British Columbia. There were two roadhouses, several stores, a bakery, a butcher shop, and even a ladies millinery and dress shop. Many built their own homes, like the cozy cabins pictured to the right. Built partly of logs and partly of lumber, these dwellings sustained many families during the hard times.

Today the area is deserted and the buildings long gone. Only the hand-piled tailings remain as evidence of the quantities of gold taken out of Lightning Creek.

Seen here at Wingdam (top) in 1900 is John Fleming, owner of the property, driving a team, with Harry Jones, a well-known miner from the 1860s, on his left. Jones, still resident here in 1927, stands in front of his cabin (middle). Ironically, a revitalized Wingdam (in 1934, right) was prosperous during the Great Depression.

LaFontaine Mine (below) existed between Beaver Pass and Stanley in the late 1880s. It was earlier known as the Eleven of England.

Beaver Pass House

Beaver Pass House stood, from 1863 until the 1940s, about 20 miles west of Barkerville. John Peebles, a successful miner and businessman, owned the property for 20 years after 1870. During 1869 Peebles wintered in San Francisco, where he married Helen (Ellen) Dickie of Arbroath, Scotland. John and Ellen had two sons, one of whom was William. William married Alice Wright at St. Saviours Church in Barkerville on December 8, 1902. This photograph of Beaver Pass House (below) was taken on their wedding day. In the picture are William Peebles, his bride Alice,

and his brother, James D. Peebles. In the back of the sleigh is a hired Chinese cook. The inset photo, taken in San Francisco in 1881, shows Ellen Peebles, mother of the groom.

The unique latticed two-storey verandah and roof were added when the Peebles hired John Strand to revitalize the building in the 1890s.

By 1930 the Gardner family had added a barn and sawmill (above), and, while they later lived in Quesnel, Beaver Pass was where a family lumber business first began.

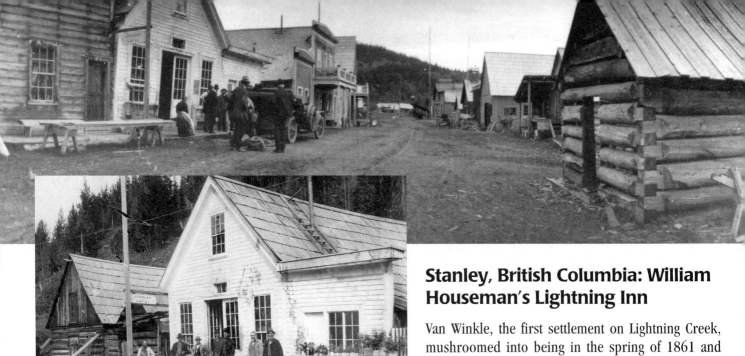

Stanley, British Columbia: William Houseman's Lightning Inn

Van Winkle, the first settlement on Lightning Creek, mushroomed into being in the spring of 1861 and continued to flourish until 1870, when it was overshadowed by a new mining community named Stanley, located a mile and a half downstream. At this time several of the hotels and boarding houses in Van Winkle were moved down the creek to Stanley, including the Yorkville Saloon and Hotel, owned by William W. Houseman. Houseman, also known as the "Duke of York," was a local character. Over six feet tall, with a commanding voice and military bearing, he claimed to have been in the Queen's Own Guard in London. Houseman, who had moved his Yorkville Saloon from Van Winkle to Stanley in the 1870s, renamed it the Lightning Hotel.

Through the years the building changed hands many times until, in the early 1900s, it was taken over by John Williams and his wife Hannah (who was known across the country for her mouth-watering pastries). A fire destroyed the original hotel in 1923, at which time Williams moved in several buildings from the defunct La Fontaine Mine, a few miles away.

A street scene in Stanley, circa 1920 (above). The Stanley Hotel (inset) operated from 1871 to 1940, when it was torn down.

The remains of William Houseman's Lightning Hotel (below), the only building left in Stanley. William Houseman is shown in the inset. When the original building burned down in 1924, the owner at that time, John Williams, moved several buildings in from the defunct La Fontaine mine and called his establishment the Lightning Inn.

Cameronton: Janet Morris Allen's Pioneer Hotel

Also known as Scotch Jennie, Janet Allen arrived on Williams Creek with her first husband, John Morris (a storekeeper), in 1862. It was not long before she gained a reputation as a nurse among sick and injured miners, and, kind and compassionate as she was, she soon became a much-beloved local citizen. After John died, probably of typhoid, Janet married William Allen, a miner on Dunbar Flats, on June 12, 1865. Janet was one of the few businesswomen in the area, and she owned several properties and hotels on both Williams and Lightning Creeks.

The Pioneer Hotel, first operated by Mr. and Mrs. J. Cameron at Richfield, was sold to Janet in 1865. As Richfield became overshadowed by Barkerville, Janet moved the hotel down the creek to Cameronton.

On September 4, 1870, as Janet was driving her buggy back to Barkerville from Dunbar Flats, her horse got too close to the edge of the road at Black Jack Canyon and went over the bank. Janet died three days later of a broken neck. On the day of her funeral the flags were flown at half-mast, and all business houses remained closed. At the service held in St. Saviour's Church a few days later, many a tear was shed and many a testimonial was given.

Taken during the late 1860s, this photograph is of Janet Allen's frame-built Pioneer Hotel at Cameronton, a community that became part of Barkerville. Standing outside the front door is Janet and the Rankin brothers, Donald and James, who were local miners.

Below, this Charles Gentile photo shows how buildings along Cameronton's main street backed onto the placer claims along the creek.

End of the Road

Ultimately the road must end. At varying times along the gold-rush trails, prospecting activity focused on creeks that today bear few signs of their glory years. Grouse Creek (above left) long bore the markings of early claims and displays the classic log shacks of the day. Richfield (left), the first settlement on Williams Creek, is captured by Charles Gentile in 1865, as is Mary's Ville (below left) and Van Winkle (bottom left). In Van Winkle the barren hillside resulted from the demand for logs both for homes and pit props for underground mining.

Above right sits Wells, the last Cariboo gold-rush centre. The Cariboo Gold Quartz Mine (top right) established this town in the 1930s. With the financial crash of 1929 and the start of a devastating depression, things looked pretty grim in the gold country around Barkerville. However, prospectors Elmer Armstrong and Fred Wells were determined to prove their theory that the nuggets of Barkerville came from a body of ore that was buried nearby. There were many doubters, including the BC Department of Mines. After ten years of hard work, Fred Wells and several investors formed the Cariboo Gold Quartz Company Ltd. (which operated the Cariboo Gold Quart Mine) in 1930. The mine soon employed 150 men and, out of this, came the company town of Wells.

During the next 20 years the population grew to 4,500, and the mine was successful beyond anyone's imagination. Between 1935 and 1943 over $1.6 million was paid out. The rich faults of Cow Mountain eventually yielded over $40 million in gold. The last mine closed in 1967, and during the 1970s and 1980s the population of Wells declined to only 200. Then, with the encouragement of several resident artists and entrepreneurs, other artists and artisans began to take up residence in the empty buildings. The Island Mountain School of Arts began to operate as a summer school in 1977 and now offers winter courses as well. Today Wells is an incorporated community of several hundred. It is supported by tourism and forestry and boasts a growing community of artists, resort operators, and cabin crafters.

Barkerville, 1868

While other townsites enjoyed brief popularity, the lore of the Cariboo gold rush will forever be tied to Barkerville. But even here history has proven that the greatest enemy of the pioneer town is fire. In mid-September 1868, Frederick Dally, professional photographer, had recently arrived on Williams Creek to capture the mood of the gold rush. He got more than he bargained for. Only days after some of these photos were taken, he and thousands of others heard that horrible shout: "Fire!" His famous street-scene photos (top) have been widely reproduced, and his panorama shots (middle) show the valley looking up Williams Creek. On September 17, after fire had devastated the entire town, the valley was in ruins and Dally, who had managed to save his equipment, pointed his lens at the only building left standing (lower right).

Barkerville: Twentieth Century

Over the years the British Columbia Archives and Records Service has gathered a rich collection of visual records that enable one to view the evolution of BC communities. Often the work of unknown photographers, as is the case on this page, these photos, along with the willingness of pioneer families to donate their treasures to public archives, have allowed both the province and the Cariboo Wagon Road communities to depict their rich history. Above left, Barkerville at the turn of the century; above right, Barkerville near the outbreak of the First World War.

Mr. Andrew Kelly and Mrs. Elizabeth Hastie Kelly, owners of the Kelly Hotel in Barkerville. In 1929 one could still tinkle a tune on an original gold-rush piano (below) at the Kelly Hotel (left).

By 1928, with the Depression still in full swing and a world war at hand, Barkerville was little more than a skeleton of its former self. In the 1960s it would be restored, and it now constitutes a marvelous tribute to British Columbia's heritage.

Nuggets on Canvas: Artists Along the Cariboo Road

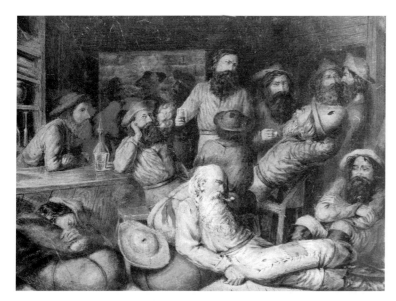

A number of artists, both professional and amateur, have left us their impressions of early British Columbia. This 1862 W.G.R. Hind painting (top left) portrays an exhausted group of Cariboo miners in an unnamed roadhouse. Above is an 1860s E.M. Richardson sketch of Richfield, the first community on Williams Creek. Below is John Innes's *The Discovery of Gold in Williams Creek in 1861*. Lower left, a rendering by an unknown artist, a sternwheeler docks at the 29 Mile House. To the left the new bridge at Quesnel Forks is captured by Frederick Whymper in 1863.

Photo Credits

Photographers like Frederick Dally, Richard and Hannah Maynard, and Charles Gentile travelled into the Interior intent on making a living with a relatively new device — the camera. This was an age when both equipment and development techniques were cumbersome.

While our earliest images come from painters and sketch artists, the most compelling and descriptive work comes from photographers. Among their innovations were stereo images — creative if somewhat contrived attempts to portray the great canyons and landscapes of the BC interior. On this page is Richard Maynard's stereo photo of the wagon road through the Fraser Canyon.

We wish to acknowledge their contributions as follows:

Leif and Eva Grandell, Studio Grandell, Quesnel (Front cover u), Mrs. Aiken (82 u); Barkerville Historic Park G-439 (87 b); BC Heritage Trust (42 b); *British Columbia, 1912*, H.J. Boam and A.G.Brown (26 u) (28 bl) (29 b) (60 mrb, br); *Canadian Mining Journal*, Oct. 1939 (34 b); Carson family collection (27 ul); Coldwell family collection (28 ul, ml); Conn, Bob (74 b); Cornwall family collection (37 mrb); Cunningham family collection (50 u); Dougherty family collection (44 b); Eden, Roy (32 b) (38 b); Felker family collection (58 ul); Fletcher, Mrs., Orville (58 b); Forbes family collection (7 b) (50 m) (54 br) (56, ul, mr, br); Gardner family (87 u); *Halfway to the Goldfields*, Lorraine Harris (26 ur) (27 ur); Hamilton, Ethel (70 mr, b); Heritage House collection (5 inset), (19 bl, br) (26 m) (73 u) (78 inset) (84 u) (93 br); Hooker, Allen (9, ul) (10 ml); *Illustrated London News, 1859* (25 b); Leeson, Ben (33 m); Lillooet Land Record Office (29 mr); Lillooet Museum (21 ur, b) (27 br); Livingston family (83 b); Locke family (84 b); Lytton Heritage Society (15 m,b) (16 bl) (17 top 4) (18 b); Mackenzie, Mrs. Olive (65 ul, ur); Memories of an Art Dealer (76 bl); National Archives of Canada C-88902 (37 mru); Patenaude Back cover photos, (13 ur) (19 ul, ur, m) (20 b) (21 ul) (23 m, b) (25 ul) (27 br) (28 mr) (30 bl, br) (36 m, b) (37 u) (40 mlu) (42 u) (44 u, m) (47 ul) (48 mr) (51 br) (53 b) (62 mr) (69 m) (71 u) (72 b) (74-75 u) (75 bl) (76 b) (80 m) (81 m, b) (82 br) (83 m) (84 m) (88 br) (90 ul) (93 ul); Peebles, George (87 inset); Pollard family collection (48 u); Prior family collection (72 ur); Prior, Emily (70 ml); *Quesnel Advertiser*, 1916, (82 m); Quesnel and District Museum and Archives (78 ur) (82 inset, bl); Quesnel City Archives (80 b); Rankin, James (66 ul, ur, b); Roberts, Dr. J. (60 ur); The "Northern Pictorial," 1958 (31 u); Vancouver Public Library 12874 (5, b) 3264 (14 ml) (50 br); *Williams Lake Tribune* (30 u) (57 m) (66 mr)

British Columbia Archives: A-03908 (Front cover b), B-00883 (4), G-00779 (5 ul), ZZ-95319 (6 ul), F-9992 (6 ur), D-00104 (6 bl), H-00608 (7 ul), PDP 101 (7 um), G-00251 (7 ur), 15032 (8 u), PDP-01782 (8 b), A-00683 (9 b), D-08238 (10 u), HP-95337 (10 b), D-03146 (11 ur), I-20553 (11 mr), 95319 (11 b), B-00930 (12 ul), A-03928 (12 b), A-3865 (13 ul), H-7365 (13 bl), A-3875 (13 b), A-3867 (14 ul), A-03879 (14 ur), D-01289 (14 b), A-3876 (15 ul), A-1329 (16 ul), G-03932 (16 ur), HP-95308 (16 u), A-03559 (17 b), A-01973 (18, ul), 58563 (18 m), G-03767 (20 ul), I-22310 (22 ul), A-09064 (22 u), 9631 (22 bl), I-51577 (22 br), H-01666 (23 ul), 28169 (24 ul), A-02327 (24 br), H-00638 (26 b), G-06725 (29 ul), E-06867 (31 m), E-06873 (31 b), F-08642 (32 ul), G-3543 (32 um), G-03187 (32 ur), 66365 (33, u), HP 763 (34 u), HP-20603 (35 ul), A-02046 (35 ur), A-3962 (35 um), A-03568 (35 bl), G-00784 (36 u), G-00783 (37 b), G-3575 (38 ml), C-09985 (38 ur), C-8207 (39 u), A-3484 (39 b), 57620, E-01243 (40 u), (40 mlb), F-07594 (40 bl), A-01645 (40 bm), H-00234 (40 br), A-3914 (41 u), 22174 (41 m), A-3913 (41 b), HP 3385 (43 ul), H-7366 (43 um), A-02110 (43 u), A-03503 (43 mr), E-03334 (43 b), A-03504 (45 u), 54078 (45 m), A-03505 (45 b), 758 (46 u), E-05434 (46 ml), 15860 (46 bl), E-05210 (46 br), 8790 (47 ur), 9569 (47 b), D-02606 (48 b), D-09300 (49 u), E-05501 (49 mr), H-00841 (49 ml), C-05398 (49 br), A-02246 (51 ur), ZZ-95308 (51 mr), E-05504 (51 ml), A-03896 (51 bl), H-00494 (52 ur), G-00791 (52 m), 10942 (52 br), I-46664 (53 ur), HP3322 (53 ml), B-01722 (54 ul), I-51576 (54 ur), 10261 (54 b), C-07559 (55 u), A-3068 (55m), E-09115 (55 b), A-03899 (56 bl), E-6874 (57 ur), I-21221 (57 b), C-08591 (58 ur), 60219 (59 ul), B-00937 (59 ur), A-01085 (59 mr), G-00396 (59 mr), D-06353 (59 b), 10262 (60 mru), 84642 (60, bl), B-01216 (61 ur), B-01198 (61 ml), B-01199 (61 mr), B-01215 (61 b), E-01433 (62 u), E-09988 (62 ml), G-7075 (62 inset), E-09962 (62 b), F-00220 (63 u), E-09986 (63 ml), E-09967 (63 mru), D-00078 (63 mrb), E-01432 (63 b), C-09870 (64 ur), (64 mr), (64 bl), A-03907 (65 b), 10270 (67 ul), A-03909 (67 mr), 95318 (67 b), ZZ-95312 (68 ul), ZZ-95263 (68 ur), A-03908 (68 b), C-04391 (69 u), A-03911 (69 b), (71, m), HP 9548 (71, b), H-06259 (73 inset), 9974 (73 b), 10474 (73 ml), A-05191 (74 ul), 09806 (75 mr), HP-22333 (76 ur), 84647 (77 ml), H-01467 (77 ur), E-06884 (77 b), B-01189 (78 mr), F-06844 (78-79 b), D-00747 (79 u), (80 u), 27222 (81 u), 29412 (83 u), G-06710 (85 ur), F-02209 (85 ml), HP-10461 (85 b), HP-50844 (86 ur), F-05611 (86 mr), E-04510 (86 br), F-00896 (86 b), 59767 (88 u), 50842 (88, ml), C-03799 (88 inset), 10154 (89 u), 10501 (89 b), 10165 (90 ur), 15274 (90 ml), G-00796 (90 ml), 10505 (90 bl), A-03557 (90 br), A-02050 (91 ul), HP94113 (91 ur), A-03748 (91 ml), A-00355 (91 mr), A-03750 (91 bl), C-05929 (91 br), B-09514 (92 ul), C-09297 (92 ur), A-03766 (92 ml), 56420 (92 mr), A-04793 (92 bl), A-03767 (92 br), PDP-00112 (93 ml), PDP-00102 (93 ur), PDP-00112 (93 ml), HP-73384 (93 bl), F-09587 (94 ur).

Code: u=upper, b=bottom, l=left, r=right, m=middle.

Back Cover photos (starting at top left clockwise): Ashcroft Manor (From Cariboo Gold Rush, Heritage House); Quesnel Forks, 1973 (Patenaude); Sam Prior's roadhouse at Little Lake, 1997 (Jack Nelson); The Gold Quartz Mine at Wells, 1970s (Patenaude); Foster's Bar, halfway between Lytton and Lillooet, very famous mining bar in 1858 (Patenaude); Keithley Creek Ranch House, 1997 (Jack Nelson); W. J. Anders Roadhouse, Alexandria built in 1896 (Patenaude, 1997); Cottonwood House prior to restoration in 1976 (Patenaude); Chinese Masonic Hall, Barkerville (Patenaude); Frank Mooney's cabin, Quesnel Canyon (Patenaude).

Index

The Author

Branwen Patenaude moved to British Columbia with her parents and brothers in December of 1941. Born in Shanghai, China, where she led the sheltered life of a British schoolgirl, her life changed dramatically when her family moved to West Vancouver. Always interested in writing, Branwen has now completed her story of the roadhouses along British Columbia's early gold-rush trails with the publication of *Golden Nuggets: Roadhouse Portraits along the Cariboo's Gold-Rush Trail*, which illustrates with pictures the stories she wrote about in Volumes 1 and 2 of *Trails to Gold*. She has succeeded in enlarging our understanding of pioneer life in the Cariboo during the last century.

Golden Nuggets completes the author's roadhouse trilogy
and the publisher's tribute to the grand history of the Cariboo Wagon Road.

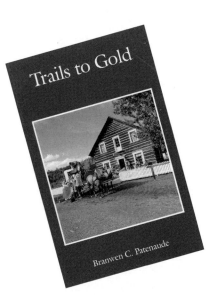

ISBN 0-920663-35-4
$14.95

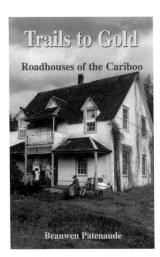

ISBN 1-895811--09-0
$18.95

ISBN 0-9690546-0-2
$19.95

Readers who want to further their knowledge of the events and people who laid the foundations of settlement in central British Columbia will find a wealth of information and entertainment in these three books, all of which are available at BC book retailers, by special order at quality bookstores everywhere, or from Heritage House. International customers may choose to order through Internet retailers www.bcadventure.com and www.cascadiabooks.com.